FASCINATING FUNGI
OF THE NORTH WOODS

Written by

CORA MOLLEN & LARRY WEBER

Illustrated by

RICK KOLLATH & BONNIE WENBORG

Kollath+Stensaas Publishing
394 Lake Avenue South, Suite 406
Duluth, MN 55802
Office: 218.727.1731
Orders: 800.678.7006
info@kollathstensaas.com
www.kollathstensaas.com

FASCINATING FUNGI *of the* NORTH WOODS

Printed in the United States of America: Duluth, Minnesota by Service Printers.
10 9 8 7 6 5 4 3 2 1 First Edition

Graphic Designer: Rick Kollath
Editorial Director: Mark Sparky Stensaas

ISBN-13: 978-0-9673793-9-5

ACKNOWLEDGEMENTS

The best way to learn about the local mushrooms and other fungi is to take frequent walks in the woods during late summer and autumn. Having an expert with you helps, and I thank some wonderful teachers of workshops that have helped me identify fungal finds. Cora Mollen (my co-author), Anne Small, Mike MacCall and Tom Volk have all given their expertise to mushroom classes I've attended. The Minnesota Mycological Society was able to help identify several of my photos. The best way to learn is to teach, and the seventh grade natural science students at the Marshall School in Duluth, Minnesota have helped me learn through their many questions. I always appreciate their enthusiasm. Also several garden clubs and the Hartley Nature Center have allowed me to speak about mushrooms.

As usual, Mark Sparky Stensaas did his terrific and patient editing, while Rick Kollath and Bonnie Wenborg provided the excellent and detailed illustrations. My wife, Frannie was supportive in letting me pursue this activity. Have a great fungi walk!

Larry A. Weber
September 6, 2006

I am grateful to my daughter, Anne Small, for her knowledge and advice which helped shape the texts, and for her computer know-how, which was indispensable. I want to thank all the members of the Northstate Mycological Club, for putting into my hands, over the years, thousands of North Woods mushrooms for discussion and study. Each member contributed to the broadening of my understanding of fungi and their role in the natural environment. Special thanks to the photographers among them, whose images captured the elements of mushroom's form and color that influenced my descriptions of various species. Thanks to educators, Pat Folgert, Carol Lanphear-Cook, Dana Richter, Daniel Czederpiltz and Stephen Nelsen. I am particularly grateful to Sparky Stensaas, Larry Weber and Rick Kollath, who gave me the opportunity to contribute to this book. It was from the start their idea, and is the fruit of lots of planning and personal effort on their part.

Sincere thanks to the experts and authors whose writings have provided grounding and substance for the descriptions in this mushroom guide: George Baron, Gary N. Lincoff, George W. Hudler, Alexander H. Smith, Alan and Aleen Bessette, Kent and Vera McKnight, Tom Volk, David Fisher, Oscar K. Miller, David Arora, Roger Phillips, Verne Graham, Michael Kao, Bryce Kendrick and Steve Nelsen.

Cora Mollen
September 1, 2006

CONTENTS

To Frannie,
my companion in life and on many mushroom walks.

And

To the students, faculty and staff at the Marshall School in Duluth, Minnesota
where I have been privileged to teach for the last 30 years.

Larry

To my husband Roy,
who encouraged the writing and was admirably patient with my piles of
books, scatterings of notepaper and hours of focus on the fungi; and to a son
and daughter whose enthusiasm for their natural surroundings caught hold of
me, and eventually brought me to the study mushrooms.

Cora

MUSHROOMS, an INTRODUCTION

What is a Mushroom?

The structure that we call a mushroom, the umbrella-shaped growth in woods, yards and parks, is only the reproductive part (sometimes called the **fruiting body**) of a much larger fungal organism. While these fleshy parts sometimes grow huge or in big clusters, they are only a portion of the fungus—the part that holds the spores. In this sense, they could be compared to an apple on a tree and, like picking the apple from the tree doesn't harm the tree, so picking a mushroom does not hurt the whole fungus.

Fungi (plural of fungus) are a very large and diverse group of organisms. They are neither plant nor animal. Like the plants, they appear to have parts such as roots, stems and branches and they are non-mobile. But unlike green plants, they cannot make their own food and so need to act like animals to get required nutrition from other sources. Modern classification treats fungi as its own kingdom though very old texts will call fungi plants.

Not all fungi are mushrooms. The word "mushroom" is often used in describing any of various fungi with fleshy fruiting bodies. This means that fungi such as molds, mildews and yeasts are clearly not mushrooms, but in a wide interpretation, any fleshy fungi; including puffballs, brackets, corals, morels and cups may be called mushrooms.

Since gilled fungi tend to be a large and common group, this book will divide all those listed as either gilled or non-gilled. Gilled fungi are the mushrooms that hold these blade-like growths, called gills, under the cap. Non-gilled fungi are all the rest: boletes (pore mushrooms), tooth mushrooms, brackets, corals, puffballs, jellies and sac fungi.

Mushroom Parts

Most of us think of a mushroom as an umbrella-shaped structure sticking up from the ground. But the part that we see is only the fruiting body (reproductive stage) of the mushroom. Most of the fungus is under ground in long thin

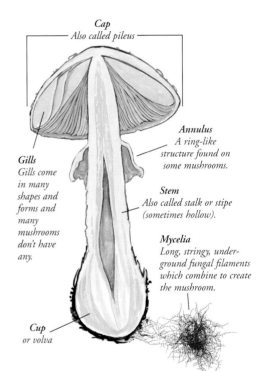

Cap
Also called pileus

Annulus
A ring-like structure found on some mushrooms.

Gills
Gills come in many shapes and forms and many mushrooms don't have any.

Stem
Also called stalk or stipe (sometimes hollow).

Mycelia
Long, stringy, underground fungal filaments which combine to create the mushroom.

Cup
or volva

growths called **mycelia**. This, as well as the entire mushroom anatomy, is composed of minute hair-like structures known as **hyphae**.

The most obvious part of the mushrooms is the cap. **Caps** are often flat and round, but they can be conical, bell-shaped or vase-shaped too. They vary in color and may be brown, gray, white, yellow, red, purple or any other color in the rainbow. Many have patches or warts on the surface that show what's left of the **veil** that once surrounded the immature mushroom (the "button") when it first grew above ground.

Under the cap are the **gills**; blade-like parts upon which the **spores** grow. Seen only with a microscope, the spores develop on tiny club-like structures called **basidia**. It is from these that the mature spores will drop and disperse. Gills sometimes attach to the stem at forty-five degree angles (**adnexed**), at right angles (**adnate**) or extend down the stalk (**decurrent**). Others have gills not even touching the

GILL ATTACHMENT

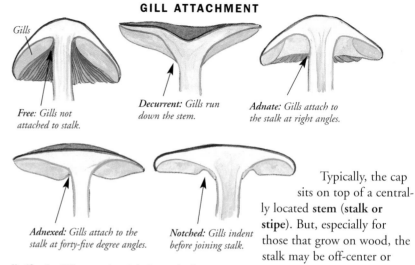

Gills

Free: Gills not attached to stalk.

Decurrent: Gills run down the stem.

Adnate: Gills attach to the stalk at right angles.

Adnexed: Gills attach to the stalk at forty-five degree angles.

Notched: Gills indent before joining stalk.

stalk (**free**). Gills may be tightly packed together or widely spaced. In place of gills some mushrooms have **teeth**, **spines** or they have tubes with holes called **pores**. All of these serve a similar function, as do the gills.

Typically, the cap sits on top of a centrally located **stem** (**stalk or stipe**). But, especially for those that grow on wood, the stalk may be off-center or even non-existent. Stalks vary in size and thickness. Many species of mushrooms have a ring (**annulus**); a band-like growth around the stalk.

The **ring** is what is left by a **partial veil** (a growth connecting the cap to

COMMON MUSHROOM CAP SHAPES

Flat   *Round*   *Bell-shaped*   *With Central Knob*   *Depressed*   *Conical*   *Vase-shaped*

TYPES OF GILLS

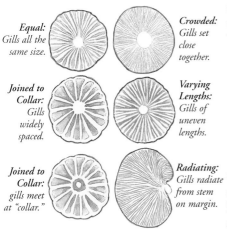

Equal:
Gills all the same size.

Crowded:
Gills set close together.

Joined to Collar:
Gills widely spaced.

Varying Lengths:
Gills of uneven lengths.

Joined to Collar:
gills meet at "collar."

Radiating:
Gills radiate from stem on margin.

called **spores**. These spores may drop from the undersides of a cap or other type of spore-bearing structure. The spores serve these purposes:

1. They are reproductive and capable of growing a new organism.

2. They are agents of dispersal.

3. They are able to go dormant for long periods until favorable conditions allow for growth.

When finding such favorable conditions—usually moisture and enough nutrients—spores germinate by growing a single filament (**hypha**). This soon proliferates to a mass of tissue (**mycelium**) that is able to penetrate into substrates; usually dead plant material. This vegetative growth may last for months or years until proper conditions are present to begin forming fruiting bodies. The reproductive phase starts when a hypha from one mycelium merges with another. This may be female and male or merely two different strains. The mushroom grows from this union.

Basidial Mushrooms
Knotted forms of hyphae begin to push above the ground. The young mushrooms, sometimes called buttons, may

the stalk which covers the developing gills). It gets torn by the developing mushroom and remnants stay on the stalk as a ring. Some species have a cup (volva) at the base of the stalk. This cup stays with the mature mushroom as a sign of the earlier universal veil that covered the entire emerging button stage. For many mushrooms, we only see the cap, gills and stalk. A few others also have rings and cups.

Mushroom Life Cycle
Mushrooms reproduce by forming small, usually single-celled structures

MATURITY OF A TYPICAL BASIDIAL MUSHROOM

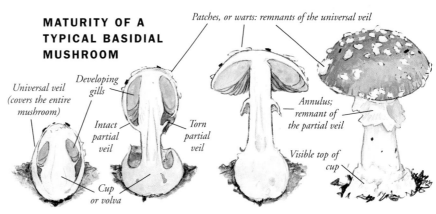

Patches, or warts: remnants of the universal veil

Universal veil (covers the entire mushroom)

Developing gills

Intact partial veil

Torn partial veil

Annulus; remnant of the partial veil

Visible top of cup

Cup or volva

Emerging button stage

Mature fruiting body

BASIDIAL FUNGI

Spores develop on club-shaped basidia.

Spores (highly magnified)

Basidia

Basidia in ridges of outer surface

Basidia in loose inner tissue

Basidia along gills

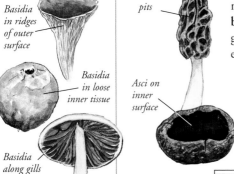

Basidia in tubes

Basidia on "teeth"

ASCIAL FUNGI

Spores develop in tube-shaped asci.

Spores (highly magnified)

Asci

Asci in pits

Asci on inner surface

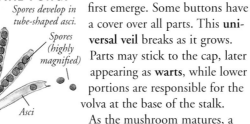

Fleshy fungi break down into two groups based on how their spores are produced.

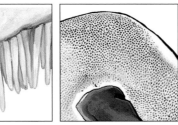

In place of gills some mushrooms have teeth or spines (left) or they have tubes with holes called pores (right).

look like chicken eggs when they first emerge. Some buttons have a cover over all parts. This **universal veil** breaks as it grows. Parts may stick to the cap, later appearing as **warts**, while lower portions are responsible for the volva at the base of the stalk.

As the mushroom matures, a new growth of spores develops on minute, club-shaped organs called **basidia** which cover the sides of the gills. Usually, four spores grow on each basidium. A mushroom's many gills provides surface area for millions of spores to form and to be dispersed.

Most fleshy fungi produce spores on basidia (**Basidiomycota**). These include the gill mushrooms, tooth mushrooms, pore mushrooms, brackets, puffballs, corals and jelly fungi.

Ascial Fungi

Others produce spores in sacs called **asci** (singular: **ascus**). These **Ascomycota** are often called **sac fungi**. Members of this group include the morels, cup fungi, dead man's fingers, jelly babies and lobster fungi. With maturity, these sacs open and spores are shot into the air. A cloud of spores can be produced by bumping these fungi as often happens with wind or rain.

Slimy Sex

The life cycle of the **slime molds** (**Myxomycota**) is different from the Basidiomycota or Ascomycota. It is now believed that they are not fungi at all. Most of the time, they live hidden in well-rotted wood or leaves. When moisture and temperature allows for fruiting, they put out a slimy mass of protoplasm (**plasmodium**) that may travel to an appropriate site to reproduce. The amoeboid movement is slow, but quite noticeable, often after a summer rain. As they move, they will engulf organic particles as nutrients. Once established, the plamodial stage becomes the sporangia

SYMBIOTIC MUSHROOM/TREE RELATIONSHIP

Mycorrhizae (fungal "roots") take carbohydrates from the tree's roots in exchange for soil nutrients the tree can't get by itself.

The mushroom is only the fruiting body of the mycorrhizae; these small fibers make up the main organism.

Tree roots

that forms tiny fruiting bodies covered with spores.

Ecology and Habitat

Once a fungus begins growing a mycelium, it needs to get nutrients. For mushrooms, it is usually one, or a combination, of three methods. Most fungi are **saprophytic**—feed on dead material, usually plants. A large number are **mycorrhizal** or mutualistic in their relationship with plants, including trees. A few are **parasitic**, whereby they gain nutrients from another living organism.

Eaters of the Dead

Saprophytic mushrooms, also called **saprovores**, use enzymes to break down dead matter and use the available biotic material to carry on their existence.

The dead and decaying matter is usually some form of wood: logs, branches, twigs, wood chips, sawdust, or it may even be dead parts of a living tree such as the outer bark and inner wood. Others gather nutrition from rotting leaves, needles, manure, pine cones or even other mushrooms. Moisture or wet conditions are needed to carry on such action.

Partners to the End

Mycorrhizal, or **mutualistic** relationships frequently exist with trees, often these are specific. Small hyphae, called mycorrhizae are the basis of this partnership. These form a mantle or sheath around the minute tree rootlets. Here a net of hyphae develop and they exchange needed nutrition. Fungi obtain sugars from the tree, while the tree gets nutrients and increased water uptake in return. With such a deeply established relationship, the mushrooms can only grow around the appropriate trees. This symbiosis is easy to note when observing the same species of mushrooms at the same place for many years.

Selfish Friends

Parasitic fungi are highly variable and may exist on a huge number of hosts, including animals, even humans. Some **parasitic mushrooms** attack trees. Being a successful parasite means not

Saprophytic mushrooms obtain nutrients by using enzymes to break down dead and decaying plant matter.

Parasites live off a host plant, endangering the host's health as it grows. The tree may eventually die but in the process create new habitats for many other organisms.

killing the host quickly. Many of these parasites live on a host for years and eventually weaken it to the point of killing it.

Some take nutrition and water from the plant while others make toxins. The surface mushroom is only the fruiting body of a mycelial growth that may go on throughout much of the body of the host.

Where Fungi Live
Because of their relationship to trees, either saprophytic, mycorrhizal or parasitic, mushrooms are most common around them. They thrive in deciduous, coniferous or mixed forests but can also be found in parks, yards, on wood chip trails or on stumps where trees used to grow.

Mushrooms can also be found in open fields or lawns. Those feeding on animal dung thrive while a few others take advantage of dead plant material. Bogs and swamps, where a continuous amount of moisture is regularly available, harbor their own specific mushroom types as well.

Collecting Mushrooms
Ideally, we would all be able to identify all the mushrooms we find in the field. Because of the huge variety of mushrooms, this is hard to do and so we often need to collect some and bring them home for a closer look. Remember that when you collect a mushroom, you are collecting only the fruiting body and not hurting the entire underground growth of mycelia. Even so, it is best to take only a few mature specimens.

Most collectors find that picnic baskets make excellent mushroom carriers. Plastic buckets or paper bags have been used too. Each specimen should be put into a small paper bag, waxed sandwich bag or waxed paper. Don't use plastic bags—they tend to hasten decay.

A Palm Pilot, small notebook or three-by-five cards are useful to record data such as habitat, type of trees nearby, whether it is growing singularly, scattered or in clusters and any other pertinent information. Many collectors place the notes directly in the bag with the mushrooms.

Most mushrooms can be cut off, dug out or removed from woody substrates with a knife. It is wise to put a colorful flag or cloth on the knife to keep it from being lost.

The majority of mushrooms in our region have their fruiting time in late summer or early autumn. Collecting in August or September is nearly always a successful venture. Their growth and development is highly influenced by the weather: going out two to five days after a significant rain may be the best time. But even during dry years, with some searching fungi can be found.

Mushroom Identification
Look for a combination of traits when identifying mushrooms, including cap shape, size and color; how gills are

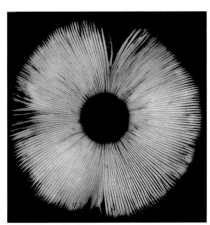

Spore print of an Amanita.

attached to the stalk; stalk texture, length, diameter, shape and color; whether there's a ring around the stalk or a cup at the base; what color the flesh bruises when cut; if the gills exude latex when cut. In addition, we should record the habitat, type of substrate, if the mushrooms grow singly, scattered or in clustered groups and date. Now consult this book in addition to others listed under Titles of Interest.

Making Spore Prints

Though all these criteria work well for determining the mushroom's family or genus, we often must take identifica-tion one step further and make a spore print. In gilled mushrooms, spores grow on the gills under the cap. It is from here that the spores fall. Spores are species-specific and can be highly effec-tive in identification.

Making a spore print is easy and though procedures vary, this method works well. Select good mature speci-men to use. Take off the cap by cutting through the stalk at the site where they meet. Put the cap on paper with gills down. A half-black-half-white piece of paper works best if you don't know whether the spores are dark or light. The cap is then covered with a glass or cup. This limits air movement so spores fall directly onto the paper. The mush-room cap is then left in this position for two to six hours—preferably overnight.

The resulting spore print on the paper is valuable for determining the mush-room's genus or even species. Many books are put together based on the color of the spore print. In this book we place an icon of the color of the spore print next to all the gilled fungi and boletes. Anyone seri-ous about further identification of mush-rooms will need to collect some, bring them home and make spore prints. Though they work best for gilled fungi and boletes, they can also be made with chanterelles, tooth fungi, corals and brackets.

HOW TO MAKE A SPORE PRINT

1. Remove the stalk and place the mushroom gill-side down on a piece of paper.

Note: you can tape together white and black paper if you don't know if the spores will be light or dark.

2. Cover the cap with a glass cup or bowl.

3. Leave the cap in position 2-6 hours or even overnight (ideal).

4. Voile! A spore print.

A Key to the Most Common Fungi Groups

Typical Mushrooms (with cap & stem)

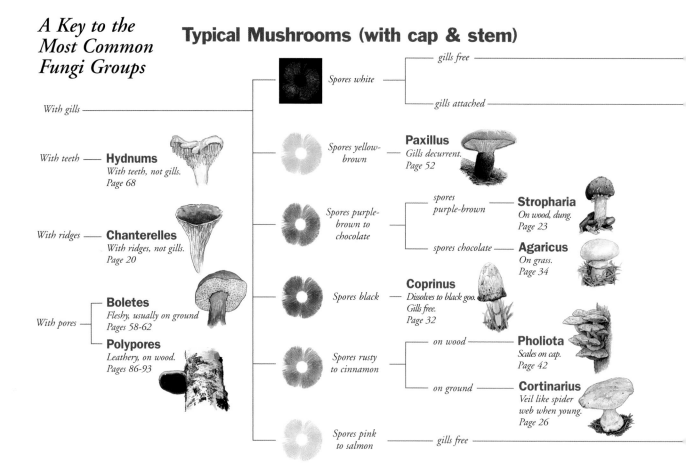

Spores white
— gills free
— gills attached

With gills

With teeth — **Hydnums**
With teeth, not gills.
Page 68

Spores yellow-brown — **Paxillus**
Gills decurrent.
Page 52

With ridges — **Chanterelles**
With ridges, not gills.
Page 20

Spores purple-brown to chocolate
— spores purple-brown — **Stropharia**
On wood, dung.
Page 23
— spores chocolate — **Agaricus**
On grass.
Page 34

With pores ⎰ **Boletes**
Fleshy, usually on ground
Pages 58-62
⎱ **Polypores**
Leathery, on wood.
Pages 86-93

Spores black — **Coprinus**
Dissolves to black goo.
Gills free.
Page 32

Spores rusty to cinnamon
— on wood — **Pholiota**
Scales on cap.
Page 42
— on ground — **Cortinarius**
Veil like spider web when young.
Page 26

Spores pink to salmon — gills free

*Based on a key in North American Mushrooms by Orson Miller Jr. 2006.

Amanita
Volva present.
Pages 12-15

Lepiota
No volva.
Page 35

Hygrophorus
Waxy. Often bright colors.
Pages 29-31

Russula
Brittle flesh.
Pages 16-18

Lactarius
Exudes latex when cut.
Page 24

Armillaria
*Clusters at base
of trees*
Page 50

volva present ——— **Volvariella**
On wood.
Page 47

volva absent ——— **Pluteus**
On ground.
Page 48

Atypical Fungi

Corals
Page 69

Jellies
Pages 69, 82

Bird's-Nests
Page 78

Stinkhorns
Page 73

Puffballs
Pages 74-77

Earthstars
Page 77

Morels
Page 63

False Morels
Pages 64-66

Cups
Page 79

**Clubs,
etc.**
Pages 70-73

Black Knot, etc.
Page 96

Hericiums
Pages 94-95

THE QUESTION OF EDIBILITY

Wild mushrooms can be the most delectable addition to a meal, but some mushrooms are poisonous, and they may resemble edible species. Eating them may make you sick or, in very rare instances, kill you. It is your responsibility to identify any wild fungi with 100 percent certainty before you eat it. If at all possible, your first few fungi forages should be with a knowledgeable and experienced mycologist.

Enthusiasm for mushroom hunting is often spurred by the hope of finding some wild delicacies for the table. Such enthusiasm must be moderated by care, experience and education. There's no need for a phobic fear of wild mushrooms, but it's important to be aware that certain mushrooms contain toxic compounds. Some of these toxins may be life-threatening; others are less dangerous, but capable of giving an unwary eater some very unpleasant moments. Only those mushrooms that are positively identified as good edibles should be eaten. A person may be guided by cultural familiarity with certain mushrooms. Formal classroom and field study with a knowledgeable teacher and use of detailed guide books can provide a basis for making accurate identifications. Some mushrooms are distinctive and well-known edibles and make a good starting point for beginners who intend to try wild mushrooms as food. Mushrooms, like other foods, can evoke individual allergic reactions, so an apt motto is "proceed with caution." Start with tiny portions to see how YOUR body reacts. The choice to eat wild mushrooms is an individual one. The individual who makes that choice is responsible for the consequences. This book is not intended to be a guide to edibility. Eat at your own risk.

Check the Titles of Interest for other books on identification and edibility of mushrooms.

HOW TO USE THIS BOOK

We've written this book to pique the interest of all nature lovers who come upon fungi in their forays afield. Often overlooked and much maligned, our North Woods fungi are a fascinating group. In these pages you'll meet a puffball that can be as big as a basketball, an *Amanita* that Viking warriors ingested before battle and the world's largest living organism.

We could not include all the species of fungi found in the North Woods—there are literally thousands of species—but we tried to include the mushrooms you're likely to notice in the field. We not only included very common species but also not-so-common species that are either uniquely shaped, huge, colorful or just plain bizarre. LBMs (little brown mushrooms) were ignored completely; even experts cannot agree on their classification. We also skipped such annoying fungi as Athlete's Foot and cheese mold. Sorry.

Fascinating Fungi of the North Woods is not arranged by color or phylogenetic order but rather is divided into six easy-to-remember categories [Listed on the upper left hand page of each spread.]:

➤ **Gilled on Ground**
➤ **Gilled on Wood** (rotten logs, living trees, wood chips)
➤ **Gilled on Other** (pine cones, leaves, animal dung)
➤ **Non-gilled on Ground**
➤ **Non-gilled on Wood**
➤ **Non-gilled on Other**

Within these categories, fungi are arranged by genus and similar forms. When you find a fungus, first try and put it into one of the above categories. [You may have to scrape away some soil to tell if certain mushrooms are indeed growing on rotten wood just below the duff layer or just arising from the ground.] Note any characteristics and grab your copy of *Fascinating Fungi* to find your fungus. Happy hunting!

We use the most well known common name and the most recent scientific name to identify each species.

Check here for the category of mushroom (e.g. Gilled on Ground.)

Inset illustrations highlight unique features of that fungus.

Size icons show the range of cap widths and stalk heights.

Phenograms let you know when that fungus may be found in the field.

Stylized icons show gill spacing (from below) and gill attachment (side view). [See introduction for explanation of terms.]

Captions point out identification traits to look for in the field.

This icon shows the color of a typical spore print. Shape, of course, will vary.

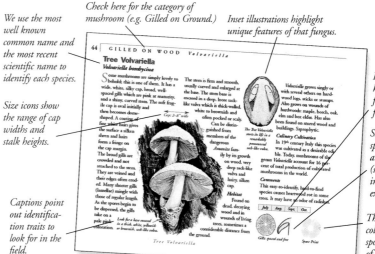

GILLED *on* GROUND

Gilled fungi are the stereotypical mushrooms that we all started drawing in second grade; they have a stalk and a cap with gills underneath.

More specifically they have spores are attached to miniscule club-shaped organs called basidia on the gills. There are thousands of species and colored like the rainbow: orange, purple, red, white, blue, green and purple. We've only included the most well-known and gaudiest species.

Be sure to check the base of the mushroom to make sure that it is growing from the soil and not attached to rotten wood. If so, check the next section "Gilled on Wood."

Fly Amanita
Amanita muscaria var. *formosa*

We tend to think of Fly Amanita as a mushroom with a bright red cap speckled with white. While this is certainly true in the Rocky Mountains, Alaska and Pacific Northwest, in the North Woods it is normally yellowish-orange with white specks. The white flecks on the cap are actually remnants of the white veil that covered the developing mushroom. A bulbous stem base hides just below the surface soil. Gills are whitish, crowded and not attached to the stem. The gills are

White "scabs" are actually remnant patches of the veil that once covered the developing mushroom.

Cap: 3–10" wide

A yellow-orange cap is the signature of the variation formosa found in the upper Midwest and Great Lakes region.

Stem: 3–7" tall

Caps may be as large as a dinner plate.

Look for the diagnostic ring on the stem.

Fly Amanita

| June | July | Aug. | Sept. | Oct. |

crowded; some are full length and others half-length. Ring is high on the stalk and the volva is mostly gone at the base.

Habitat

Scattered to grouped, usually gregarious, in woods under aspen, poplar, birch, pine, spruce and fir. Mycorrhizal with birch, aspen and spruce. They may be found in mixed forests but are usually on acidic soils.

A circumpolar species that spans North America, Scandinavia and Russia. Found in North America from Alaska to Labrador and south to North Carolina and the Rocky Mountains.

Fungal Fly Swatter

The name Fly Amanita comes from the belief that a saucer of milk with a cap of *Amanita muscaria* can stun or kill flies. Even in Norway it is called *Rød Fluesopp* or "red fly mushroom."

Gills: crowded and free

Spore Print

Viking Vice

Rumor has it that the Vikings of the eleventh and twelfth centuries revered *Amanita muscaria*. One of its side effects is said to be brief periods of superhuman strength sometimes followed by coma-like sleep and possibly death. Could this have been the Vikings' secret in battle?

Alice in Wonderland

Toxins atropine and muscarine combine in Fly Amanita to cause symptoms of intoxication and on rare occasions, death. Symptoms would be much more severe if the two toxins did not tend to neutralize each other. Lewis Caroll, author of *Alice in Wonderland*, was a known experimenter with drugs. The white-spotted red mushroom illustrated in his book is most likely Fly Amanita. Is it possible that Caroll took Amanita and experienced its hallucinogenic effects? Would this explain small things appearing large in the story…and other bizarre details?

Lovely but Lethal

A full 90 percent of all fatal mushroom poisonings have been attributed to Amanitas and their deadly amatoxins. Amatoxins cause severe, life threatening illness. If even a small portion of a mushroom that contains amatoxins is eaten, the powerful toxins act on the cell system of the body blocking vital production of new cells. Liver and kidney failure and death can result. The symptoms of the poisoning are delayed; occurring six to eight hours after the poisonous mushroom was eaten. Then nausea, vomiting, fever and tremors take hold. These may be bad enough to cause hospitalization. But the symptoms are temporary and may be passed off as a case of simple food poisoning. (That's why recent consumption of mushrooms should always be mentioned to the attending doctor) Three to six days later, however, there are symptoms of liver failure. By that time, the toxins have done much internal damage to liver, kidneys, intestines as well as heart and brain.

Destroying Angel
Amanita virosa

This tall, robust, pure white mushroom has a pristine appearance. The large cap is convex then nearly flat with a raised center and clean, unlined margin. Its surface is smooth without ornamentation and has a satiny, shimmering quality. The white gills are close and free. They are narrow to somewhat broad and sometimes with a powdery look. Shorter gills mix with full-length gills.

The partial veil is membranous and breaks to form a thin skirt-like ring on the upper stem. The ring is delicate, gets tattered and sometimes disappears.

The stem is thick, tapering upward and with a small ball-like base. A large white volva encases the stem base. The volva's upper edges are free from the stem and often scalloped. It may be necessary to dig into the soil to uncover the volva. The mushroom has a yeast-like odor.

Habitat
Usually found in mixed woods, but fruiting also occurs in open areas with sandy acidic soil and an edging of trees.

Pernicious Poisoner
This mushroom is said to be the most deadly mushroom in eastern North America. Besides *Amanita virosa*, there are two white, dangerous look-alikes, *A. bisporigera* and *A. verna*. The three can only be distinguished from one another by chemical and microscopic exam. Unfortunately, to date, there is no specific antidote to amatoxins. Treatment involves attempts to stabilize and sustain the victim and to clear the toxins from the body (see sidebar).

Physician, Heal Thyself
French physician and researcher, Dr. P. Bastien developed a method of treatment that he used to save a number of amatoxin victims. Later, to test and verify the efficacy of the treatment, Bastien twice consumed amatoxin-con-

Cap: 2-5" wide

Spore Print

Look for tattered, thin skirt-like ring on the upper stem.

Stem: 3–8" tall

Angel of Death

You may have to dig for it, but look for the large white volva that encases the stem base. It is often free at the upper edges and may be scalloped.

| June | July | Aug. | Sept. | Oct. |

taining mushrooms and then set to cure himself. That's dedication to research! The

Gills: crowded and free

Bastien method is the chief amatoxin treatment used in France.

It is a three-part treatment: 1. Intravenous injections of one gram of vitamin C twice daily; 2. Two capsules of nifuroxazide three times daily; 3. Two tablets of dihydrostreptomycin three times a day. Penicillin, fluid control and electrolyte balance supplement the treatment.

The Meixner Test

The easy way to test a mushroom for amatoxins is called the Meixner Test. Draw a circle on newsprint paper. Press the liquid out of a piece of fresh mushroom into the circle and allow it to dry. When dry, put a drop of concentrated hydrochloric acid on the circle. If amatoxins are present, a blue color will develop within 20 minutes. The more amatoxins present, the quicker the blue reaction.

Tawny Grisette
Amanita fulva

A classic beauty with simple "tailored" lines. It has a broadly bell-shaped cap, long tapering stem and pale sheath-like volva. The cap is orange, orange-brown to red brown with a smooth rather glossy surface and deeply lined margin. Mature caps are flat with

Spore Print

a raised center. The white to cream-colored gills are broad, closely packed under the cap and free from the stem. The mushroom's firm stem is tapered upward. It has a white, even surface with faint hints of cap color and a covering of very fine white hairs. There is no ring. A large, showy volva encloses the stem base. It is white to tan in color and its tissue is soft, delicate and easily torn.

| July | Aug. | Sept. |

Habitat

Amanita fulva is found in or near bogs; also in low damp areas of coniferous and deciduous woods.

Gills: crowded and free

Cap: 1–3" wide

Tawny Grisette

Stem: 3–4" tall

Note prominently grooved margin and lack of ring

Typical Amanita trait; look for the large white volva.

Why so Brittle?

All Russulas are characterized by a special brittleness. Mushrooms are composed of long cylindrical filaments called hyphae. These create a fibrous, reasonably sturdy tissue. Russula fruiting bodies have another component—large, thin-walled spherical cells called sphaerocysts. These cells mix with the hyphal filaments, often forming groupings like rosettes or islands in the mushroom tissue. The round sphaerocysts are physically less stable than longer thread-like hyphae. Their considerable presence in Russula bodies makes the mushrooms vulnerable to snapping.

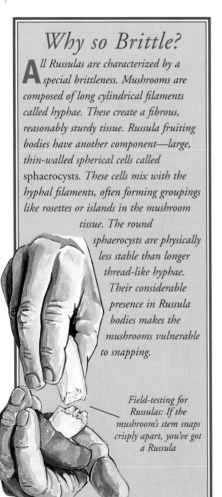

Field-testing for Russulas: If the mushroom's stem snaps crisply apart, you've got a Russula

Yellow Swamp Russula
Russula claroflava

Let's start by saying up front that Russula identification is at best an iffy proposition. Even mycologists can't agree on species characteristics under a microscope! That said, this mushroom has a bright, chrome-yellow to lemon-yellow cap, white to pale ochre gills and white stem. The stem develops noticeable gray to black areas as the mushroom ages. An important feature for identification is its tendency to very slowly turn gray and then black after it is cut or bruised. This color change can be seen in all parts. There are other yellow-capped russulas that turn gray to black when injured, but they do so very quickly. *Russula lutea*, another yellow-capped mushroom, does not show any color change when bruised and has a sticky cap.

The flesh will slooowly turn gray and then black when bruised.

Habitat
You find Yellow Swamp Russula in swampy woods (surprise!), and often under birch.

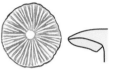

Spore Print   Gills: adnexed to almost free

This species has a dry yellow cap while the closely related species, Russula lutea, *has a sticky yellow cap.*

Cap: 2–4" wide

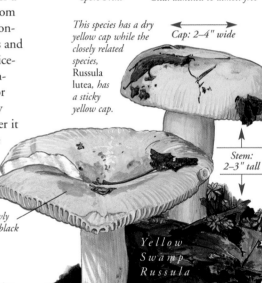

Stem: 2–3" tall

Yellow Swamp Russula

| July | Aug. | Sept. | Oct. |

Emetic Russula
Russula emetica

This is a standout in the piney woods and sphagnum bogs where it appears. The mushroom cap is cherry to blood red.* Below are close, broad, white gills and a pure white stem. The cap may be somewhat slimy or sticky and the red may fade out in rain or with age. The whole mushroom body is so brittle that it easily breaks in your hand. Emetic Russula is not found in deciduous woods. The not-so-pleasant name, *Russula emetica*, suggests the mushroom's chemical make-up can cause vomiting (*emetic* means "that which induces vomit").

Habitat

Solitary, scattered or in groups in woods. In sphagnum moss under conifers or in mixed woods. Rarely on rotten wood. Mycorrhizal.

July	Aug.	Sept.	Oct.

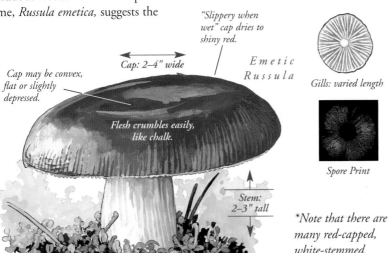

"Slippery when wet" cap dries to shiny red.

*E m e t i c
R u s s u l a*

Cap may be convex, flat or slightly depressed.

Cap: 2–4" wide

Flesh crumbles easily, like chalk.

Gills: varied length

Spore Print

Stem: 2–3" tall

*Note that there are many red-capped, white-stemmed Russulas in the woods.

Field and Lab

Russulas can be relied upon to add color and interest to any North Woods trail walk from early summer to late fall. These common mushrooms are typically tidy in appearance with smooth, rounded to level caps, neat white gills and white cylindrical stems. The range of their cap colors is truly impressive, spanning the spectrum from white to red to purple-black to yellow.

There are so many look-alike Russulas that, with a few exceptions, field identification is impossible. It takes study in the lab to verify their scientific names. There is one important feature that Russulas share; all have minute starchy ornamentation on the surface of their spores. Under a microscope these literally light up in blue when moistened by a drop of the iodine solution called Melzer's reagent. This so-called amyloid reaction is an important feature of the Russula.

Short-stalked White Russula
Russula brevipes (formerly *Russula delica*)

The Short-stalked White Russula is a very common North Woods mushroom. It is often found at the edge of footpaths in pine needle duff and wood debris, its white cap barely emerging from the litter. In fact, it is often found by seeing a hump in the moss or duff of the forest floor—a "mushrump," if you will. When taken in hand, dirt and needles cling to it giving a scruffy appearance. Once the dirt is removed you have a very robust, firm mushroom, creamy white overall.

The cap of this species is dry and made felty by a mat of tiny white fibrils. The smooth edges of the cap tend to turn down and with age the cap takes on a funnel shape. The thin gills are crowded under the cap and descend the stalk slightly. Take a careful look at the gills. Note that they are alternately long and short, that they fork and are joined by veins.

Unlike the white *Lactarius* species (Milk Caps), this mushroom does not exude latex.

Russula brevipes may be transformed into a completely different looking mushroom by the parasitic fungus, *Hypomyces lactifluorum* (nicknamed "The Lobster," see page 97), which engulfs the entire mushroom in a bright orange over coating.

Habitat
Scattered or in groups under conifers or mixed woods.

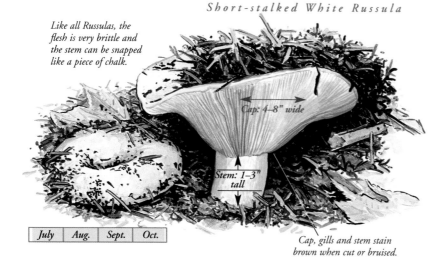

Short-stalked White Russula

Like all Russulas, the flesh is very brittle and the stem can be snapped like a piece of chalk.

Cap: 4–8" wide

Stem: 1–3" tall

| July | Aug. | Sept. | Oct. |

Cap, gills and stem stain brown when cut or bruised.

Gills: varied length and decurrent

Spore Print

Rooted Collybia
Xerula furfuracea (Oudemansiella radicata)

A tall, attractive mushroom with a long rooting stem base. The cap is convex to flat with a distinct, central knob. The honey-colored to gray-brown surface has a thick, rather elastic skin (cuticle) that is sunken and wrinkled around the wide, rounded knob. The cap margin has a translucent quality. Broad, rounded, pure white gills are a bright contrast to the darker cap. Gills are attached initially but later cede and hang free. There is a mix of regular length and shorter gills.

The long, sturdy stem tapers upward. Stem may be somewhat twisted with

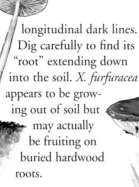

X. furfuracea *is easily identified by its white spore print, slender stature and very distinctive long tapering "root" that extends into the ground.*

longitudinal dark lines. Dig carefully to find its "root" extending down into the soil. *X. furfuracea* appears to be growing out of soil but may actually be fruiting on buried hardwood roots.

Habitat
Solitary, scattered or in groups on ground near old stumps or decaying deciduous logs, especially beech. Saprophytic.

Cap: ½–4" wide

Stem: 3–10" tall

Hard to miss: Note the unusually long, graceful, stem that tapers toward the top.

Rooted Collybia

Spore Print

Gills: varied length, well separated and free

May	June	July	Aug.	Sept.	Oct.

Chanterelle
Cantharellus cibarius

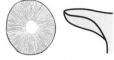

"Gills:" varied length and decurrent

You know it's summer when fresh crowns of Chanterelles push up to brighten pine needle beds and grassy woodland slopes. Everything about this mushroom is appealing. The cap is solid, smooth and colored a warm egg-yolk yellow. The white flesh is firm, but breaks crisply.

Chanterelles do not have true gills. Shallow blunt folds, colored like the cap, curve from cap margin to well down the stalk. These pronounced folds fuse and split in an irregular pattern. The orange-yellow stalk is fairly wide, tapers downward and provides a solid base. Because of its fibrous nature it can be peeled apart into strings.

Chanterelles have a fruity odor that suggests apricot.

Spore Print

Similar Species
False Chanterelle (*Hygrophoropsis aurantiaca*, next page) has a fine felt-like covering of the cap, an earthy smell, thin and hollow stem and crowded gills. Jack O' Lantern (*Omphalotus olearius*, see page 41) grows in clusters at the base of trees or on dead wood, stumps or roots.

Habitat
Scattered to clustered on ground under oaks and conifers (spruce and pine); mixed woods. Mycorrhizal with spruce and pine and some deciduous trees.

A World Favorite
The Chanterelles are known and appreciated worldwide. The French call it *Girolls*, the Germans know it as *Pfifferling* and in Scandinavia it is sold dried in packets for a camping soup mix. Chanterelles are known globally as one of the best forest edibles. If you relish mushroom dishes, make yourself familiar with this species. Its flavor is excellent. It fruits abundantly, keeps well and is reasonably free from insect pests.

The quantity and quality of its fruitings make it a target for commercial harvest. and their international commercial value likely exceeds a billion dollars annually. In the Pacific Northwest, commercial harvest of this mushroom is a multimillion-dollar business.

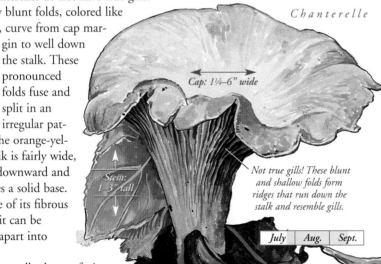

Chanterelle

Cap: 1¼–6" wide

Stem: 1–5" tall

Not true gills! These blunt and shallow folds form ridges that run down the stalk and resemble gills.

| July | Aug. | Sept. |

False Chanterelle
Hygrophoropsis aurantiaca

Bright orange gills and nicely uplifted margin make this an attractive find. The cap is flat, then funnel-shaped with an orange and brown color mix. The center is dark, the margin pale. The cap has a suede-like surface, especially over the center, and a thin, soft, white to orange-tinted flesh. Narrow, very crowded gills add a flash touch of orange. They are repeatedly forked, blunt-edged in young specimens, but become blade-like as the fruiting body matures. There is an orange-brown, finely hairy stalk which is often off-center, sometimes nearly lateral. Stalk may be twisted and curved. It is enlarged at the base.

Cap: 1–3" wide

False Chanterelle

Stem: 1–4" tall

Aug.	Sept.	Oct.	Nov.

False Chanterelle: look for true, thin, blade-shaped gills.

Chanterelle look-alike?

Though called "False Chanterelle" because it vaguely resembles *Cantharellus cibarius* (the Chanterelle), a number of features help differentiate them. The egg-yolk yellow Chanterelle is solid, more robust and fleshy. *H. aurantiaca* is orange to orange-brown with soft, thin flesh. The Chanterelle has thick, round-edged ridges or folds, set widely apart. The gills of *H. aurantiaca* are narrow, very crowded and, in mature specimens, blade-like. The fresh Chanterelle has a pleasant, fruity odor. *H. aurantiaca* does not.

Habitat

Found on the ground in pine needle duff and woody debris and on conifer logs and stumps.

Gills: narrow, crowded and decurrent

Spore Print

Forest Funnel Cap
Clitocybe gibba

When mature, this tidy, pinkish-tan mushroom with its smooth pale stem suggests a small wine cup. The cap becomes deeply depressed, almost funnel-shaped. The gills that line the underside of the up-turned cap are crowded, white, descending a short way onto the stalk. This mushroom often appears in early summer before other gilled mushrooms make their appearance.

Habitat
Solitary and in groups in decaying leaves, especially under oak. Saprophytic.

Gills: varied length and decurrent

Spore Print

Like some other mushrooms and plants, C. gibba releases minute amounts hydrogen cyanide into the atmosphere.

Cap: 2–3" wide

Stem: 1–3¼" tall

Base often with cottony mycelial growth.

July	Aug.	Sept.	Oct.

Leaf litter adheres to the stem base.

Funnel Cap

The Miller
Clitopilus prunulus

This mushroom is said to have an odor like fresh ground meal and so is commonly called "The Miller." The dull white to grayish cap is irregular in

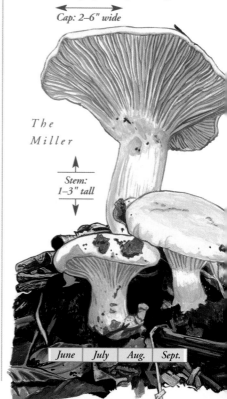

Cap: 2–6" wide

The Miller

Stem: 1–3" tall

June	July	Aug.	Sept.

shape with a sunken center and an inrolled margin that becomes flaring, lobed and wavy with age. The cap surface is suede-like. The flesh is white and firm. The gills are fairly well-spaced and descend deeply down the stalk. Gills are white, but once the spores mature, they take on a pinkish hue. The stalk, colored like the cap, has a dry, somewhat cottony surface. It is vertically ridged and often has a swollen mid-section. It is typically off-center.

Spore Print

Habitat
The Miller fruits alone or in scattered groupings in grassy areas in open woodlands. It is frequently found under juniper. May grow from rotting boards on buildings.

Gills: decurrent and closely spaced

Wine-cap Stropharia
Stropharia rugosoannulata

Large maroon-red to chestnut-brown cap, wide, violet-tinted gills and a white stem with a unique ring, make this mushroom eye-catching. The cap presents a dry smooth surface. With age, cracks may develop on the surface and the margin often splits. Whitish at first, the gills later take on a violet-gray color and finally become brownish-black when the mature spore are released.

The firm, smooth stem has a bulbous base surrounded by white mycelial threads. In unfavorable weather, the stem wall may break to form curls of stem tissue. The stem has a telling feature: a large, thick, membranous ring, grooved along its upper rim. The lower section of the ring is separated into claw-like or crown-shaped points.

This mushroom is easy to cultivate

Cap: 2–6" wide

Spore Print

Stem: 4–6" tall

| June | July | Aug. | Sept. | Oct. |

Wine-cap Stropharia

The stalk holds a partial white veil that leaves a persistent membranous ring with claw-like points.

in straw or on wood chips. Masses of mushroom mycelium are developed commercially and made available to growers.

Habitat
Scattered to numerous on wood chips, mulch, straw, gardens, lawns or cultivated fields. Saprophytic.

Gills: adnate and closely spaced

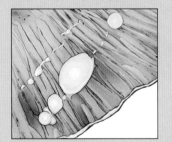
Saffron Milk Cap
Lactarius deliciosus

This sturdy mushroom with a green-staining orange cap is found in conifer territory, especially under pines. The cap is flat, centrally depressed and has an inrolled margin. Its surface, when young, is covered with a whitish bloom. It is typically shiny and somewhat sticky and is decorated by concentrically arranged salmon-orange to purple spots and streaks. Gills are pale-orange, narrow and crowded with some cross veins and forking. They often show greenish stains.

The firm stem is cylindrical, becoming hollow with age. Its surface is smooth or may have a series of spot-like depressions. Mycelium may be found at the stem base.

All parts of this mushroom stain green when injured; even the orange latex turns green when exposed to the air. You may detect a fruity odor.

Habitat
Single to scattered to gregarious in moist areas, boggy places, along streams, under conifers; especially pine. Mycorrhizal.

Spore Print

Cap: 2–5" wide

Saffron Milk Cap

Flesh stains green when bruised. Exudes orange latex when cut.

Note whitish bloom on young caps.

Stem: 1–3" tall

Gills: decurrent and closely spaced

| July | Aug. | Sept. | Oct. |

Indigo Milk Cap
Lactarius indigo

If color could define a living thing, "blue" would define this milk cap mushroom. The cap, gills and stem of a fresh young specimen are a bright, dark blue. The broad cap is depressed at the center and has a thick inrolled margin. The

Indigo-blue latex is exuded when any part is cut.

Note decurrent gills.

surface is smooth, sticky, and decorated with concentric zones of deep blue. Cap flesh is brittle, pallid with a bluish tint. As the mushroom matures, the cap color fades to a lustrous blue-gray. The deep blue, attached gills are set close together and descend the stem slightly. The rigid stem is blue to silvery blue-gray, cylindrical, hard and hollow. All parts of the mushroom stain blue-green when bruised.

Habitat
Scattered or in groups on soil in oak and pine woods.

Cap: 2–6" wide

Indigo Milk Cap

Stem: 1–3½" tall

| July | Aug. | Sept. | Oct. |

Spore Print

Gills: closely spaced

Pepper Milk Cap
Lactarius piperatus

Like others in its genus, this large cream-colored mushroom exudes a fluid (latex) when cap or gills are cut. Pepper Milk Cap has a dull, dry cap with hairless margin. The gills are extremely crowded with numerous forkings. The latex is white, sharply bitter and very hot to taste.

Habitat
Scattered to grouped on soil in deciduous woods; some in mixed forests. Mycorrhizal.

Spore Print

Gills: decurrent and closely spaced

Cap: 3–10" wide

Pepper Milk Cap

Stem: 1" tall

| July | Aug. | Sept. |

Violet Cort (Purple Cort)
Cortinarius violaceus

An exceptional woodland beauty with deep violet cap, gills and stem. Flesh is blue to deep purple. The cap becomes flattened with a low central hump and is densely covered with fibrous, violet scales. The broad gills are widely spaced and eventually take on a rusty-brown tone as spores are released. The cortina is a cobwebby partial veil that is present under the cap (see inset on next page). The stem widens toward a rounded base.

The uniform dark-violet color and dry scaly cap help set this mushroom apart from others with violet coloring. It is not, in spite of its color, a good source of fiber dye.

Cortinarius is a very large genus and may have 1000 members in North America.

Habitat

Solitary, scattered, or in groups among mosses under conifers or mixed woods: fir, pine, aspen, alder, oak. May be near decomposed logs. Mycorrhizal with conifers and deciduous trees.

Spore Print

Violet Cort

Note the fibrous scales on the cap that separate this species from the few other blue and purple mushrooms in the North Woods.

Cap: 2–4¾" wide

Stem: 3–7" tall

Sept.	Oct.

Gills: decurrent and closely spaced

Spotted Cort
Cortinarius iodes

Violet is the color theme carried out in the cap, gills, stem and flesh of this mushroom. The broadly-rounded cap is smooth and decidedly slimy when wet. It has a splattering of pale yellow spots on an otherwise violet surface.

Cap and stem slimy when wet.

Cap: 1–2" wide

The stem is often bulbous at the base.

Stem: 2–3" tall

July	Aug.	Sept.

Spotted Cort

The violet gills are attached, close and quite broad. As the mushroom matures, the gills take on a cinnamon-gray coloration due to the release of rusty-brown spores. The smooth, solid stem is, like the cap, very slimy when wet. Cobwebby veil remnants ring the upper stem. Both stem and veil are violet.

The mushroom has a pleasant odor.

Habitat

Look for Spotted Cort growing singly or in groups, on the ground under deciduous trees.

Gills: adnate and closely spaced

Spore Print

Rimmed-Bulb Cort
Cortinarius species

This mushroom belongs to a group of yellowish to orange *Cortinarius* species with an abrupt rim on the bulbous stems. Its thick, firm cap is rounded with an incurved margin. It becomes flatter with age. The cap surface is slimy when moist. The coloration of the cap varies from all yellow to ochre to orange with a yellowish margin and there are sometimes spot-like surface scales. The flesh has a radish-like odor. Yellow to ochre gills are set close together. They are attached and may be notched at the

Cap: 2–5" wide

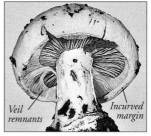

Veil remnants *Incurved margin*

Note the incurved margin, the veil remnants and how the close-set gills attach to the stem—common traits of young Corts.

stem. Eventually, gills are tinted rusty-brown by mature spores. The stout, solid stem is short with a large rimmed bulbous base. The rim is most distinct in young specimens.

Habitat

This is a widely distributed group of species that grows singly or in groups on the ground under hardwoods or conifers.

Rimmed-Bulb Cort

Spore Print

Stem: 1–2" tall

| June. | July. | Aug. |

Gills: adnate and closely spaced

Capturing a Mushroom's Color

Beautiful colors can be extracted from fungi...but not necessarily the color of the mushroom. Because some species may be poisonous, preparation of the dyes needs to be done away from the kitchen. In one large pot (not aluminum), 2-3 quarts of water and 10 grams of alum are heated. The yarns or other fibers are put into the hot (not boiling) water and set aside for one hour. Meanwhile the mushrooms (about a quart) are boiled in 2-3 quarts of water for one hour, then allowed to cool slightly. The yarns/fibers are then carefully drained and placed in the hot mushroom liquid together with the mushrooms. Steep one hour, stirring occasionally. Yarns/fibers are then carefully rinsed. Add one cup of vinegar to one rinse. Give the material a final rinse and hang to dry out of the direct sun. Get out your knitting needles!

Red-gilled Cort
Cortinarius semisanguineus

The yellow-brown fibrous cap is quite ordinary. At first, it is bell shaped. The mature cap is flat with a slightly raised center called an umbo. When the dull cap is turned over, however, there is a surprise. The gill-bearing underside sports a startling, blood-red or cinnabar coloration. The red gills are closely packed, narrow and broadly attached to the mushroom's yellow stem. The stem is pale at the top and reddish at its base. Since this is a *Cortinarius* species,

Note the distinctive reddish-colored gills.

its developing gills had been protected with a web-like covering called a cortina. The remnants of that covering form a fibrous zone on the upper stalk. You may notice a slight odor of radish when handling this fungus.

Cap: 1–2" wide

Stem: 4" tall

Habitat
The mushroom can be found in moist mixed-forest depressions where sphagnum and other mosses have taken hold. It likes the company of a tangle of blueberry shrubs.

Red-gilled Cort

Dyeing Breed

C. semisanguineus has a proven track record as a source of fiber dye. When cooked with alum as mordant it yields a yellow to red dye. A warm cinnamon-orange color is achieved when the dye is applied to various fibers including wool. Attaining dyes from mushroom species has a long history and is becoming a popular interest and occupation today. There are international fungus-fiber symposiums held at various cities around the world. In their book, *Rainbow at My Feet*, mushroom experts, Arlene and Alan Bessette explore the many facets of this fascinating subject. [See sidebar on page 28.]

Gills: adnate and closely spaced

Spore Print

Aug.	Sept.	Oct.	Nov.

Witch's Hat
Hygrophorus conicus

This mushroom's conical hat with pointed central peak earns it the common name Witch's Hat. The cap may be variously colored: bright red, red-orange or yellow with hints of green. It is thin, fragile and translucent with a smooth surface. When moist, it is somewhat sticky. The cap edge is striate and often splits as the fruiting body matures. The closely spaced yellow gills are thick, soft and waxy. They eventually become torn and unevenly frayed. There is a delicate cylindrical stem that is colored like the cap. It may be twisted and longitudinally lined. White mycelium can be seen at the stem base.

A telling characteristic of this fungus is that it blackens readily when bruised and becomes blackened with age.

Habitat

It fruits under conifers and is very common.

Cap: 2–4" wide

Spore Print

Witch's Hat

Stem: 3-6" tall

Note longitudinal lines on stem.

All of the Witch's Hat will blacken when bruised. You may find one all black in the field.

Gills: free and well spaced

June	July	Aug.	Sept.

Scarlet Waxy Cap
Hygrophorus coccineus

The form and color of this mushroom are captivating. The cap is bell-shaped early on, then flat with a central depression, and often with a widely flaring margin. The surface is an intense scarlet with some yellow tints. The flesh is fragile and yellow-orange. The waxy gills curve broadly under the cap then descend the stalk a short way. Their color is red to orange-cream. There are numerous cross veins. The hollow stalk is red with a yellow base, often curved and flattened. It grows in dense clusters—often so crowded that the caps of some individuals are deformed from pressing up against their neighbor.

Cap: 1–4" wide

Stem: 1–3½" tall

Scarlet Waxy Cap

| July | Aug. | Sept. | Oct. |

Gills appear as long triangles. Note hollow stem.

The name "waxy cap" refers to the waxy texture of the flesh if rubbed between the fingers. Hygrophorus means "bearer of moisture."

Specimens of *coccineus* tend to have an appealing originality about them: the tilt of cap, curve of gill, their variability and glow of color. They're a favorite of photographers. Peaked red-orange caps appear greasy and are in fact moist to the touch.

Spore Print

Gills: well-separated and adnexed to free

Habitat

Scarlet Waxy Caps often appear in large groups in cool moist woods. Also in depressions dominated by balsam, hemlock and pine. Sometimes grassy areas, clearings and meadows. Often is association with mosses. This species also grows under the lofty shadows of Coastal Redwood trees in California.

Cap: 1–3" wide

White Waxy Cap

Stem: 2–6" tall

*Cap and stem are **very** slimy when wet.*

White (Ivory) Waxy Cap
Hygrophorus eburneus

The soft–fleshed cap is flat with an incurved margin. As the mushroom matures the margin tips upward. The cap is smooth and bright white.

The white gills are well spaced and waxen and may bruise yellow. The slender stem is smooth and white and narrows downward to the base. In some specimens you may detect a strong odor of sage.

The feature note for *Hygrophorus ebruneus* is its very slimy cap and stem. As mycologist David Arora aptly puts it, This is the "slipperiest and slimiest gilled fungus among us."

Habitat
Single to scattered to gregarious on leaf litter of deciduous woods and grassy areas. May also appear in mixed pine-oak, pine-beech woods. Appears to be mycorrhizal with beech on fertile soil.

Spore Print

Gills: decurrent and well-separated

Aug.	Sept.	Oct.	Nov.

Parrot Waxy Cap
Hygrophorus psittacina

The parrot mushroom is one of the gems of moist, mossy woodlands, catching filtered sunlight in its colorful translucent cap and stem. It begins with a bright green bell-shaped cap, green gills and stem. As it matures, a variety of lovely pastels intermingle with the green tones. If you take one in your hand, you will be amazed at the range of colors, all highlighted by the thin waxen flesh of the mushroom. It is uniquely beautiful.

Parrot Waxy Cap

Cap: ⅜–1½" wide

Stem: 1½–2½" tall

Gills: Attached

Spore Print

July	Aug.	Sept.	Oct.

Alcohol Inky (Tippler's Bane)

Coprinus atramentarius

Tight crowds of these glossy, lead-gray mushrooms appear in gardens, on stumps and in grassy places enriched by buried woody debris. Young caps are egg-shaped with margins puckered and pressed against the stem. At maturity, the mushrooms are bell-shaped with a grooved, splitting margin. Cap flesh is thin and pallid. The gills are set close together, broad and initially white in color but turning dark. The cylindrical, silky-white stem is hollow. A dark zone of veil material rings the lower stem.

Self-destructive Behavior

Coprinus species share a unique method of dispersing their spores. The self digestion process progresses from the margin to the stem, freeing the mature black spores. Left behind is a forlorn bunch of stems and a twisted, sheeting of inky, oil-like material.

Cap: 1½–3" wide

Alcohol Inky

Stem: 1½–6" tall

| May | June | July | Aug. | Sept. | Oct. |

One of the earliest gilled fungi of the season.

Coprinus *mushrooms begin dissolving from the margin.*

Note the dark zone of veil material

Booby Trap

Mycologist Bryce Kendrick calls *C. atramentarius* a "booby trap for drinkers." Coprine is a unique amino acid contained in this fungus. It is not itself a poison, but it causes considerable problems for anyone who consumes an alcoholic beverage within 48 to 96 hours of eating the mushroom. The unfortunate drinker will face the outset of alarming symptoms; flushing of face and neck, swelling and numbness of hands and face, rapid heartbeat, tingling extremities, nausea and vomiting. Coprine, which persists a long time in the diner's system after eating, blocks the body's metabolism of ethyl alcohol, stopping the process at the acetaldehyde stage. Acetaldehyde is the poison causing the symptoms. It should be noted that the symptoms of coprine poisoning disappear on their own without treatment.

Habitat
Clustered in grasses and woody debris and near buried wood in lawns; wood chips. decaying deciduous stumps. Bases of unhealthy trees, especially aspen and poplar. Park, gardens, along streets, residential areas, city dumps.

"Autodeliquescence:" these inky caps will soon be liquid. This liquid was once used for writing ink!

Gills: free and closely spaced   *Spore Print*

Shaggy Mane
Coprinus comatus

The cap of the young mushroom is tall, column-like to oval with a smooth, white to ochre surface and a margin that is pressed in against the stem. The maturing mushroom expands to become bell-shaped. Its margin is lined and tattered. The cap's white outer skin (cuticle) breaks into broad, overlapping scales. Scale edges tend to fray and curl upward giving the mushroom a distinctive "shaggy dog" appearance. White gills are densely packed under the cap. They are free, straight and narrow. There is often a delicate pinkish tint in the gills. The silky, white stem is cylindrical and hollow.

There is a thin, movable ring low on the stem. The base of the stem is enlarged, pointed and rooting. Like other inky caps Shaggy Mane disperses its spores by a gradual dissolving of cap and gill tissue. This is an easily recognized species with its column-like form and copiously scaly cap.

It is a much sought-after and choice edible. There are no toxic look-alikes.

Shaggy Mane

Habitat
Solitary to scattered to clustered in grass, wood chips, hard packed soil, along roads and trails as well as disturbed sites: lawns, pastures, gardens, garbage dumps, compost heaps. May grow in urban or suburban settings. Saprophytic.

Gills: free and closely spaced

Cap: 1¼–2½" wide

Cap: up to 6" tall

Scaly cap surface helps distinguish this species from the Alcohol Inky.

Strong? They've been known to push up through asphalt.

Stem: 2½–8" tall

Spores black; but nearly impossible to get a print without a black gooey mess.

June	July	Aug.	Sept.	Oct.

Fairy Rings

Mushrooms drop their spores in a circular pattern and the resulting hungry hyphae expand outward, seeking nutrition. Your lawn is literally an even playing field; a substrate evenly composed of a constant and uninterrupted food supply. The "ring" of advancing mycelium expands like a ripple in a pool, finding and feasting on untapped organic matter in the soil. Depending on conditions, these rings will continue to expand, growing in circumference a few inches or a few feet every year. If the mycelium "decides" to produce fruiting bodies, the result is a fairy ring, popping up as a ring of mushrooms above the leading edge of the mycelia. The best known fairy ring mushroom is the edible Marasmius oreades, but several others, such as the Meadow Mushroom (Agaricus campestris), also follow this growth pattern.

Meadow Mushroom
Agaricus campestris

Cap: 1½–4 wide

Stem: 1–2½" tall

Meadow Mushroom

These white-capped mushrooms appear in arcs, fairy rings or scattered groups on lawns, in grassy meadows and pastures and along grassy roadsides. The smooth cap is typically dome-shaped, becoming flatter with age. The cap's center (disk) is often darkened by soft, gray-brown hairs or scales. These are especially evident during dry periods. The cap has thick, firm flesh that, at times, may be flushed with pinkish or brown tints. It does not stain when bruised. Look for frayed veil remnants; they're often found hanging from the strongly down-turned cap. Gills are free, narrow and crowded. A delicate pink coloration of the young gills is a notable feature of this mushroom. As the mushroom expands, the gills become bright pink and eventually, with spore release, they become chocolate-brown. The solid stem is short, giving the mushroom a squat appearance. The stem is dry and smooth above a narrow flimsy ring (ring often wears away). The stem surface below the ring is covered with fine fibers. Stem is white

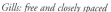

Gills: free and closely spaced   *Spore Print*

but becomes dingy reddish brown with age. There is no cup (volva) at the base. They tend to be abundant following rains and cool weather.

Supermarket Fare
Most shoppers are familiar with the typical white, fleshy mushroom sold in supermarkets. This commercially-grown mushroom is *Agaricus bisporus,* a very close relative of the Meadow Mushroom. The difference is microscopic, resting on the number of spores found on each spore producing basidia. In the case of *A. bisporus,* there are two spores per basidia; *A. campestris* usually has four spores. A bit of trivia for the common man, but important for scientifically separating the species.

Habitat
Solitary or in groups; often in fairy rings on ground in grassy areas such as lawns, meadows, pastures, cemeteries, golf courses, parks and roadsides. Saprophytic.

Aug.	Sept.	Oct.

Shaggy Parasol
Lepiota rachodes

A striking feature of this mushroom is the pattern of scales on its cap. The cap of the developing mushroom is pinkish to cinnamon-brown. As the cap grows and expands, the outer colored skin breaks apart into large, rough, curling tissues. These lie in concentric circles on an underlying pale surface. The mushroom body is large, with a thick, wide cap, broad whitish gills and a sturdy stalk with rounded base. If you cut away the cap you will see the upper portion of the stalk is hollow. The thick white ring on the upper stalk is membranous and moveable. Ring edges may be reddish-brown. The cap and stem stain yellow-orange when cut.

Habitat
Can be found singly or sometimes in fairy-ring groupings in the grass along roads and on cultivated soils.

Spore Print

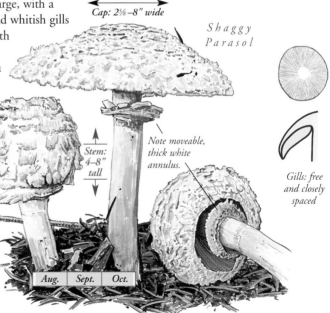

Cap: 2⅜ –8" wide

Shaggy Parasol

Stem: 4–8" tall

Note moveable, thick white annulus.

Gills: free and closely spaced

Aug.	Sept.	Oct.

Blewit

Lepista nuda (Clitocybe nuda)

Look for a generous, late-fall fruiting of *C. nuda* on damp decaying leaf piles and compost heaps. The large mounds of organic material and soil pushed to the side of shady country roads by graders are also a likely place to find groups of fruiting bodies. Color is a defining feature; the cap, stalk and gills of young specimens are a clear lilac-blue. The thick-fleshed caps have a smooth, oily surface. Mature caps are flattened, often with

Spore Print

a shallow central depression. They may develop cracks in dry weather. Eventually the caps take on a red-brown color and the thin cap margin, inrolled at first, tends to become uplifted, flared and wavy giving the mushroom a lopsided, jaunty look. Perhaps this inspired its common name Blewit (Blue Hat). Gills are broad and fade with age from lilac to pinkish-tan. They never, however, take on a rust color as do some other fungi with violet coloration.

There is no veil. The Blewit's stem is solid and fibrous, often with a bulbous base.

The base may be overlaid with whitish hairs and develop a brownish surface. You can frequently find a downy mat of violet-colored mycelium attached to the base. The mushroom has a fragrant odor of anise.

Seems to favor cool weather and tends to grow back when cut down. Due to the blue or violet cap, it may be confused with *Cortinarius*, but it doesn't have the latter's webby veil or spore color.

Habitat

Single to numerous on needle duff or leaf litter under conifers or hardwoods. Also in humus-rich ground, around sawdust, mounds of leaves, decomposing organic matter, even may grow on shredded newspaper. Also seen along paths and woods edges, beneath blackberry stems. May form fairy rings. Saprophytic.

Gills: adnate, closely spaced and sometimes notched

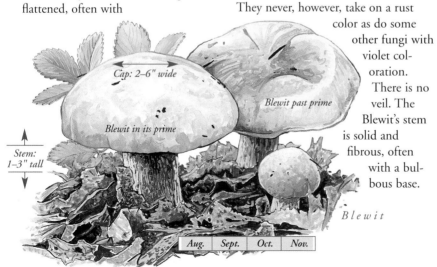

Cap: 2–6" wide

Blewit past prime

Blewit in its prime

Stem: 1–3" tall

Blewit

| Aug. | Sept. | Oct. | Nov. |

The FUNGI of LATE FALL & WINTER

October is a terrific time to observe the North Woods forests. Colorful leaves of red, orange and yellow put on a splendid display during the early part of the month but soon they will be gone, and the trees' bare branches will again be in view for the next seven months. But while looking up at the fall leaves don't forget to look down for fall fungi.

Some late season mushrooms appear on the ground near tree stumps among the fallen leaves. Peak mushroom watching time was in August and September. At that time, the woods walker could easily find up to 20 kinds. Now, only a few persist in the cooling forests.

Some of our yards may hold growths of Shaggy Mane and Alcohol Inkies (*Coprinus* species) or Meadow Mushrooms (*Agaricus* species). If the Meadow Mushrooms look familiar it may be because they are closely related to the cultivated ones we put on our pizzas and in our salads. Watch also for explosive Puffballs (*Lycoperdon* species) whose golfball-like crusty exterior can be tapped to release millions of spores. Whether we are child or adult, it is hard not to step on these brown fungi. Flattening the fungus and sending out such tiny smoke signals may seem to be hurting this growth, but we are actually helping the puffballs to do what they want to accomplish when mature—disperse their spores to reproduce. Giant Puffballs (*Calvatia gigantea*) may reach the size of a deflated basketball.

But it is in the woods that the biggest growths of October mushrooms occur. At the base of dead oaks, maples or birch, we may find large clusters of Honey Mushrooms (*Armillaria mellea*). They are highly variable in their appearance and occurrence; common some years and rare in others. On nearby tree trunks look for the golden-brown Pholiotas (*Pholiota* species). Don't forget to look up when hiking in the autumn woods as Pholiotas may grow quite high on tree trunks.

Don't give up when November blows in. Warm weather and wet ground may allow a few fleshy fungi to flourish for one last fling. But for consistent winter fungi watching, one must turn to the woody polypores known as brackets or shelves. Turkey Tail (*Trametes versicolor*) grows in colorful overlapping masses on deciduous trees. It persists all year but is easiest to see when the woods are bare. Paper Birches host several very distinctive polypores: the bulbous Birch Polypore (*Piptoporus betulinus*) and the Hoof Fungus or Tinder Polypore (*Fomes fomentarius*), which actually looks like a horse's hoof with the annual growth rings easily visible.

So don't give up on our Northern fungi in late fall and winter. They are out there. Watch for them on your next autumn hike or even on a winter snowshoe trek!

GILLED *on* WOOD

Many of our gilled mushrooms that are found on wood grow in dense clusters. Few can forget the sight of a moss-covered log sprouting dozens of orange Fuzzy Foot mushrooms.

Not all grow on downed rotting logs. Look for Sharp-scaly Pholiota, Tree Volvariella and Netted Rhodotos on the trunks of living trees.

Some gilled fungi are less obvious in their attachment to wood. Jack O' Lantern, Platterfull Mushroom and Clustered Collybia often appear to be growing out of the ground but are usually rooted in subsurface decaying wood.

One of the finest forest edibles is a gilled-on-wood species; Oyster Mushrooms are a wonderful addition to a meal when sauteed in butter. But get them quickly before the fungus beetles make a meal of them before you!

Bleeding Fairy Helmet (Bleeding Mycena)
Mycena haematopus

Well-decayed birch and oak logs host colonies of this *Mycena*. The delicate mushrooms crowd together often in tufts with stem bases joined. Mature caps are helmet-like in shape. Their color varies from purple-gray to red-brown. Cap surface is faintly lined and a hump (umbo) is evident at the cap center. The cap's thin flesh, when moist, possesses something of a translucent quality. Cap edges are scalloped and often neatly upturned. The gills are whitish becoming spotted with red and brown. The narrow, hollow stem is colored like the cap. A mass of coarse white hairs can be seen on its base. Occasionally you will find this mushroom covered by the fine, spiky threadings of the mold called *Spinellus fusiger* (see sidebar on next page).

The distinguishing feature of *Mycena haematopus* is its response to injury. Both cap and stem, when cut or broken, exude drops of blood-red latex, and hence, the common name, Bleeding Mycena.

Habitat
May be single, but usually in clusters on well-decayed wood of deciduous trees. Often on rotting birch. Saprophytic.

Cap: ⅜–2" wide

Stem: 1–4"tall

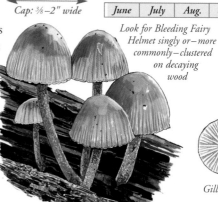

June	July	Aug.	Sept.

Look for Bleeding Fairy Helmet singly or—more commonly—clustered on decaying wood

Spore Print

Gills: varied and adnate

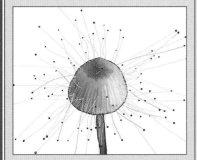
Pinwheel Marasmius
Marasmius rotula

Clusters of these small, attractive mushrooms commonly occur on decaying deciduous wood. Each delicate cap is parasol-shaped with a broad central depression. The cap surface is dry, parchment-like. A neat arrangement of radiating pleats reach almost to the scalloped margin. White gills attach to the collar on a fine, wiry, shiny black stem. Sometimes a few brown, root-like hairs are attached to the stem base.

Resurrection!
Shriveled and inconspicuous, *Marasmius* species are rarely noticed during dry weather, but after rainy periods the tiny fungi flesh out, hence the nickname "resurrection fungi."

Habitat
Several to numerous on twigs and branches of dead or decaying wood. Common on beech.

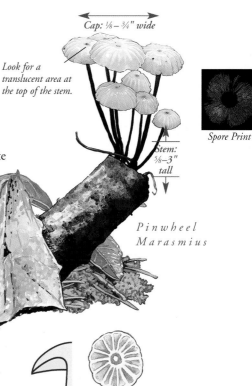

Cap: ⅛ – ¾" wide

Look for a translucent area at the top of the stem.

Stem: ⅝–3" tall

Spore Print

Pinwheel Marasmius

Gills: Adnate and attached at collar

| June | July | Aug. | Sept. | Oct. |

Fuzzy Foot

Xeromphalina campanella

Also known as Golden Trumpets, this fungus produces a veritable army of small fruiting bodies exclusively on conifer wood and conifer debris.

Look for cross-veins: small, intersecting ridges between the gills.

A tough, slender, curved stem supports the cap. It is yellow near the top and dark red-brown below with a dense tufting of long, bright tawny hairs at its base that earns it the name, "Fuzzy Foot." The individual mushroom cap is rounded to flat with a pit-like central depression. Cap surface is moist, but not slimy and colored yellow, orange or tawny brown with darker tones on the disk (cap center). Cap has thin and pliant flesh and a prominently-lined and turned-down margin. Narrow gills are set far apart and extend down the stem. They are yellow to dull orange and have cross-veins (see inset illustration).

Spore Print

Habitat

Large clusters, often numerous, on decaying and moss-covered logs, stumps and woody debris of conifers: Hemlocks, Eastern White Pines or Jack Pines. Saprophytic.

Cap: ⅛ – 1⅜" wide

Fuzzy Foot is so specialized in its choice of host that a fruiting confirms that the stump or log is surely a conifer.

Gills: decurrent and spaced

These fungi have fuzzy feet! Look for the dense tuft of hairs at the base of the stalk.

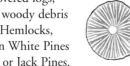

Stem: ⅝–3" tall

Fuzzy Foot

June	July	Aug.	Sept.	Oct.	Nov.

Jack O' Lantern
Omphalotus olearius (Omphalotus illudens)

This fungus produces huge clumps of sturdy, brilliant-orange mushrooms at the base of stumps and on the roots of living trees. It also fruits on buried wood. Mature caps are large, flat and depressed with a low pointed central knob. They are usually orange, but sometimes are a ruddy- brown color. The surface of the cap is smooth and streaked with innate dark fibrils. The margin is incurved, wavy and splits with age. Cap flesh is thin, firm and pale yellow. There are narrow, sharp-edged gills tightly packed under the cap. The individual gill is bow-shaped with narrowing at each end. Gills run down the stalk for some distance. The tough, fibrous stalk is dry, smooth and colored like the cap. With age the stalk surface may become downy or scaly.

Evil Jack

This poisonous species should not be mistaken for the eminently edible Chanterelle. Its sharp-edged gills, growth on decaying wood or living trees and strong disagreeable odor give it away. *Omphalotus olearius* is not only dangerous to humans but is a powerful pathogen of trees, eventually killing its host tree.

Habitat

Dense clusters on buried wood, roots and stumps of oaks and other deciduous wood. Often grows where trees have been removed. Sometimes seems to be growing from the ground. May be a parasite on broadleaf trees. Saprophytic or parasitic.

Jack O' Lantern

Cap: 2–6" wide

Stem: 2–8" tall

Called Jack O' Lantern because it may glow in the dark. But, the light emitted is greenish, not orange (see sidebar on previous page).

Inexperienced mushroomers may mistake this species for Chanterelle. But note the sharp-edged gills, dense clustered growth on wood; characteristics not shared with the Chanterelles.

Gills: decurrent and crowded

Spore Print

| July | Aug. | Sept. | Oct. |

Sharp-scaly Pholiota
Pholiota squarrosoides

Mounds of spiky, yellowish caps on scaly stems cling to living trees or hardwood stumps; clumps of 50 or more are not unheard of. The cap of the mushroom is rounded, with a low umbo. A gelatinous, sticky surface underlies stands of sharp, erect scales (veil remnants) that are scattered near the margin, but concentrated over the cap center. The brownish-orange scales are dry and have recurved tips. Older caps, which are weather-washed, may lose the scales. The white gills are crowded and attached, usually with a notch near the stem. As the spores mature the gills become rusty-brown. There is a sturdy, yellowish stem, circled near the top by a pale, cottony ring that may disappear due to the wear-and-tear of the elements. The stem top is whitish and silky. Below the ring it is covered with coarse down-curved brown-orange scales.

Habitat
Clusters found on deciduous wood, dead or alive. Also on trees, stumps and logs of birch, alder, beech and maple. Occasionally on decaying conifers. Saprophytic or parasitic.

Cap: 1–4" wide

Stem: 2–6" tall

In wet weather or in old age, the cap has a gelatinous, sticky surface with scattered dry scales.

Sharp-scaly Pholiota

Aug.	Sept.	Oct.

Gills: attached, notched and crowded

Spore Print

Scaly Pholiota
Pholiota squarrosa

"Scaly" nicely sums up the character of this mushroom. Its cap and stem are both closely covered with upright scales giving it a shaggy charm. The basic cap is pinkish-tan to straw-colored sometimes with a greenish-yellow margin. The cap is bluntly rounded when young, becoming bell-shaped in age. The scales, formed by the break-up of the cap cuticle, cover the entire surface and are persistent. The margin adds to the mushroom's shaggy appearance with its fringe of veil materials. Gills are attached, close and narrow. As the

Spore Print

Cap: 1–4" wide

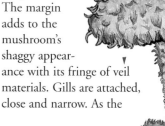

Scaly Pholiota

July	Aug.	Sept.	Oct.

mushroom ages, gills take on a greenish tint and finally become rusty-brown. The stalk is thick, tapering down to an enlarged base. A fragile, yellowish ring (or zone of shredded veiling) is found on the upper stem. The stem is smooth and solid above the ring. Below, countless down-turned scales, like those on the cap, cover the surface.

Habitat

Pholiota squarrosa fruits in tufts or clusters on the trunks, stumps and roots of hardwoods and conifers.

Gills:
attached, notched and crowded

Split Gill
Schizophyllum commune

Split Gill may be the most widely distributed mushroom in the world. It is found on every continent except at the North and South Poles. The small, gray to white, fan-shaped caps grow in groups or lines on dead branches and logs of hardwoods. The caps have a conspicuous covering of white hairs. Caps are tough and leathery with a scalloped, inrolled margin. Stemless, the

Cap: ⅜–1⅝" wide

Split Gill

May be the most widespread mushroom in the world.

caps attach directly to the wood. Gills radiate from the mushroom's point of attachment and curve outward to the margin. Gills are deeply grooved or split lengthwise (see inset illustration above). These curves and lines give the tiny fungus an attractive, arty touch. To survive dry times, the mushroom cap curls down over the gills. Once moister days return, caps quickly revive.

Note the very distinctive doubled rows: the "Split gills" are really two adjacent but separate gills.

Habitat

Solitary, scattered or in overlapping clusters on dead branches, logs or stumps of hardwood trees. May also appear on straw bales and driftwood or boards of hickory, walnut, elm or oak. Has even been found growing on animal matter: whalebones and the scar tissue of a human mouth. Saprophytic.

June	July	Aug.	Sept.	Oct.	Nov.

Fruiting June - November; Can be seen year round.

Crinkle Gill
Plicaturopsis crispa

This interesting fungus is found on dead hardwood in overlapping clusters. Caps are fan-shaped with deeply lobed or wavy margins. Mature caps have zoning of tan-brown and red-brown with cream-colored margins. The fertile underside has shallow, gill-like folds that are notably crimped (wavy). A close look will show that they are forked and are joined by numerous cross veins. Caps curl when dry. They revive and become soft and flexible in wet conditions.

Undersides: not really gills! Look for shallow, gill-like folds.

Habitat
Overlapping clusters on branches and trunks of hardwoods: beech, birch or cherry. Most often seen during or after rainy periods.

Cap: ⅜ – ⅞" wide

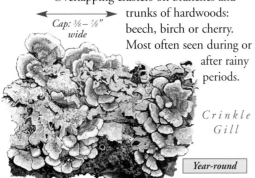

Crinkle Gill

Year-round

Oyster Mushroom
Pleurotus ostreatus

This mushroom possesses a special beauty. It flares out from the host wood singly, shelf-like, or in tight, overlapping clusters, displaying a smooth clean cap, an arching inrolled margin and a wide sweeping curve of gills. It fruits on stumps, aspen and willow snags and other decaying woods (but not usually on conifer).

Often abundant at the time when folks are busy scouting the woods for morels.

The cap is shell-shaped or fanlike and may be cream, gray or brown. The surface is moist, but not slimy and cap flesh is thick creamy-white, firm but tender. The cap is often attached directly to the wood (sessile), but a short, sturdy, curving stem may be found. It holds the cap laterally or centrally depending on where the fruiting body is positioned on the host wood. The stem has a velvety, hair-covered base.

Oyster Mushroom

Two forms may be observed. The light-capped ones grow in warmer weather, the dark-capped ones appear in cooler times.

Cap: 2–8" wide

Stem: if present, up to 1½" tall

Oyster Mushroom

When growing out of the side of a log, the stem is lateral or absent, but centralized when above the log.

The white gills have moderately wide spacing and extend down to the point of attachment. Many shorter gills are interspersed with the full length gills.

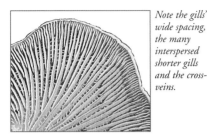

Note the gills' wide spacing, the many interspersed shorter gills and the cross-veins.

Habitat

Large clusters, often overlapping, on stumps, logs and trunks of deciduous trees, especially visible on standing dead aspens. Has been reported on elm, cottonwood, alder, oak, willow, poplar, beech, aspen and maple. Saprophytic and parasitic.

Edible Complex

This easy-to-recognize mushroom is actually part of a complex of very similar mushrooms that are hard to separate and identify, even by microscopic features. However, they are all choice edibles. Once established in a patch of woods, the Oyster makes itself at home and can be found fruiting annually.

Best to gather this mushroom quickly when you spot it, as it soon will have a compliment of shiny black fungus beetles who will ruin the caps by tunneling through them.

Look who's coming for dinner: Oyster Mushrooms are often home to prolific tiny pleasing fungus beetles (Family Erotylidae*) such as* Triplax thoracica.

Oil Eater

Oyster Mushroom spores are used in straw mats to help collect and eat oil spills. Acids and enzymes released by their mycelium breaks down the complex molecular structure of petroleum-based contaminants. They were used recently off the coast of Spain.

Spore Print

May	June	July	Aug.	Sept.	Oct.

Attack of the Killer Hyphae!

The hyphae of Oyster Mushrooms produce tiny appendages called stephanocysts which secrete a potent toxin. Nematodes (small, microscopic roundworms) which are unfortunate enough to cross paths with the stephanocysts are quickly paralyzed. Other specialized hyphae then find and penetrate the nematode's outer layer and digest its inner contents. This, of course, spells the end for the nematode but makes a tasty nitrogen snack for the fungus.

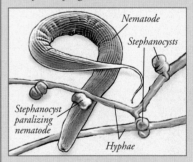

Nematode

Stephanocysts

Stephanocyst paralizing nematode

Hyphae

And not only nematodes need beware; scientists have also observed bacteria colonies being attacked. Once P. ostreatus detects a nearby colony, it sends out a very fine hyphae that penetrates the bacterial colony and forms specialized feeding cells inside. These break down and consume the bacteria, transferring the nutrients back to the main mycelial body.

Netted Rhodotus
Rhodotus palmatus

A very special find whose range seems to be limited to Northeast North America. The rounded apricot-pink to reddish cap is ornamented with a unique network of ridges and shallow pits. The flesh of the cap has a rubbery feel and appears gelatin-like. The pale pink gills are broad, connected by veins and are also rather rubbery.

The pink stem completes the con-colored array. It is tough and fibrous, off-center and typically bent. The mushroom is said to have a pleasant odor.

Fruitings do not happen every year and never occur more than once on the same wood.

Cap: 1–2" wide

When clustered, the overlapping caps often adhere to each other because of the gummy cap surfaces.

Spore Print

Stem: 1–2" tall

Netted Rhodotus

| June | July | Aug. | Sept. |

Habitat
Solitary to scattered on old dead hardwood logs, trunks or posts. Especially found on maple, sometimes elm and poplar.

Fungal Non-Conformist
This mushroom's unusual combination of features, color, netted cap surface, gelatinous flesh and its spore color, set it apart from the traditional categories, so mycologists created a new genus, *Rhodotus*, to accommodate it. *Rhodotus palmatus* is the lone species in the genus.

What's in a Name?
A mushroom's species name often focuses on a notable part of its make-up. It could be the shape of stem, special coloration, shape and character of the cap, a particular habit of growth or a specialized habitat. In the case of R. palmatus, the given name points to the likeness between the mushroom's cap with its pattern of ridges and the shape and lined surface of the human palm.

Tree Volvariella
Volvariella bombycina

Some mushrooms are simply lovely to behold; this is one of them. It has a wide, white, silky cap, broad, well-spaced gills which are pink at maturity, and a shiny, curved stem. The soft fragile cap is oval initially and then becomes dome-shaped. A coating of fine white hairs gives the surface a silken sheen and hairs form a fringe on the cap margin. The broad gills are crowded and not attached to the stem. They are veined and their edges often eroded. Many shorter gills (lamellae) mingle with those of regular length. As the spores begin to be dispersed, the gills take on a pale pink coloration.

Cap: 2–8" wide

Stem: 2⅜–8" tall

Look for a base encased in a thick, white, yellowish or brownish, sack-like volva.

The stem is firm and smooth, usually curved and enlarged at the base. The stem base is encased in a deep, loose sack-like volva which is thick-walled, white to brownish and often pocked or scaly. Can be distinguished from members of the dangerous *Amanita* family by its growth on wood, very deep sack-like volva and hairy, silken cap.

Habitat
Found on dead, decaying wood and in wounds of living trees, sometimes a considerable distance from the ground.

The Tree Volvariella starts its life in a remarkably pronounced sack-like volva.

Volvariella grows singly or with several others on hardwood logs, sticks or stumps. Also grows on wounds of hardwoods: maple, beech, oak, elm and box elder. Has also been found on stored wood and buildings. Saprophytic.

Culinary Cultivation
In 19th century Italy this species was cultivated as a desirable edible. Today, mushrooms of the genus *Volvariella* account for 16 percent of total production of cultivated mushrooms in the world.

Comments
This easy-to-identify, hard-to-find species causes heartwood rot in some trees. It may have an odor of radishes.

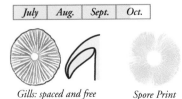

July	Aug.	Sept.	Oct.

Gills: spaced and free

Spore Print

Tree Volvariella

Deer Mushroom
Pluteus cervinus

Cap: 1–4¾" wide

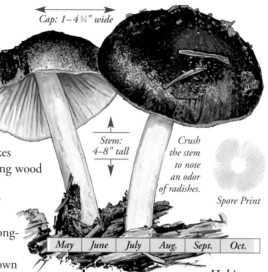

Stem: 4–8" tall

Crush the stem to note an odor of radishes.

Spore Print

May	June	July	Aug.	Sept.	Oct.

Walk a stretch of forest land where there are large quantities of downed, rotting birch logs, and chances are you will find this mushroom. It usually takes an erect stance among decaying wood and white curls of bark.

In form, the fruiting body with its dark, sweeping cap and white stalk resembles a long-handled, partially-opened umbrella. The cap is dark-brown to smoky-gray with a low central hump (umbo) and is lined radially with imbedded darker fibers. The cap is moist, but not slimy. Broad, white gills are free and crowded under the cap and soon become pinkish due to the release of mature spores. Gills are rounded in back. The long white stem is smooth and firm. At times there is a darkening of the base caused by brownish hairs.

"Free" gills are not attached to stem

Gills

Stem

Habitat

In addition to birch, *P. cervinus* can be found fruiting on broad-leafed and conifer timber.

Free Gills

This is a good species for observing what scientists call free gills. Hold a specimen, stem up, in your palm. Look down to where the stem and cap join. You can see that there is an open space around the stem and that the gills stop before reaching the stem.

Clustered Collybia
Collybia acervata

*A**cervata* means "clustered," and these little mushrooms live up to their name. When fresh and moist, the caps are a dark red-brown with paler margins. When dry or aged, they become pale tan. Caps are rounded to almost flat and very smooth. After rains they take on a water-soaked look, but are not slimy. The narrow gills are whitish-pink and the smooth, hollow

Cap: 1–2" wide

July	Aug.	Sept.	Oct.

and flexible stalk is a dark wine-brown with fine white hairs covering the lower half. Stem bases are joined and seem bound together by a thick mass of mycelium.

Habitat

Large compact groups can be found on rotting conifer stumps, logs and buried conifer wood. Sometimes appears to be growing from the soil.

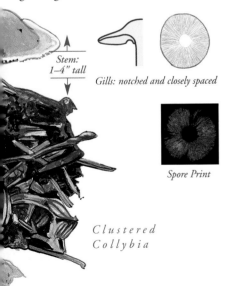

Stem: 1–4" tall

Gills: notched and closely spaced

Spore Print

Clustered Collybia

Platterfull Mushroom
Megacollybia platyphylla (Tricholomopsis platyphylla)

This mushroom is one of the earliest gilled mushrooms to appear in spring. It fruits on rotting logs, wood debris and buried wood in groups and in tufts with joined stem bases. The cap of mature specimens is silver-gray to gray-brown with smooth surface streaked radially by darker fibrils. The cap is relatively flat with sunken center and small umbo and its margin is thin, wavy and often split with age. The flesh of the cap is pliant and fragile.

The very broad, ragged-edged, white gills are adnate to notched, with conspicuous cross veining. There is no veil; the stalk is smooth, sturdy and becomes hollow with age. A scattering of flattened white hairs and grayish coloration can often be seen at the base.

The fascinating feature of this mushroom is the white, shoe-string-like rhizomorphs attached to the stalk base which are root-like and spread widely and deeply into the substrate.

Habitat

Single to scattered on well-decayed logs, stumps, wood debris or buried wood in hardwood or conifer woods. May even fruit on leaf litter. Saprophytic.

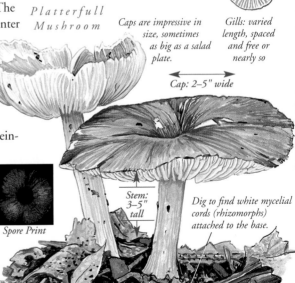

Platterfull Mushroom

Caps are impressive in size, sometimes as big as a salad plate.

Gills: varied length, spaced and free or nearly so

Cap: 2–5" wide

Stem: 3–5" tall

Spore Print

Dig to find white mycelial cords (rhizomorphs) attached to the base.

| May | June | July | Aug. | Sept. | Oct. |

Honey Mushroom
Armillaria mellea

Instead of generating food from sunlight, Indian Pipe — which is a flowering plant, not a fungus — parasitizes the Honey Mushroom that, in turn, takes nutrients from oaks and other trees.

They are called Honeys, Cinnamon Tops, Buttons, Stumpies and a myriad of other names. The mushrooms produced by the fungus, *Armillaria mellea* are sought after, gathered and eaten by thousands of folks. Probably in a mushroom popularity contest they would take top prize, at least for their quantity. The mushrooms are found in massive colonies on the stumps, buried wood and on trunks of living hardwoods, especially Northern Red Oak. Caps come in a variety of colors; honey-yellow, tan, pink-brown to red-brown. The cap's surface is covered by a scattering of brown-black, sharp, tufted hairs, with a concentration of them over the cap's central knob. These scale-like tufts are a hallmark of the Honey Mushroom. The cap is slimy when wet. Flesh is thick and white. On older caps the margin may be wavy or flaring. Often, in a dense cluster of the mushrooms, you will find lower caps covered with the dusty powder of spores released from caps above.

Gills are well-separated, white to pale yellow.

Cap: 1–4" wide

Stem: 2–6" tall

Honey Mushroom

Aug. | Sept. | Oct.

They are attached to the stem and somewhat decurrent. In older mushrooms the gills may be stained yellow to rust. The stalk is pith-filled and later hollow. It is thick, tough and fibrous, often with a bulbous base. The white membranous ring, or remnants of it, should be found on the upper stalk.

Habitat

Grows in clusters at base of trees, near stumps; living or dead. Grows on either conifers or hardwoods, but more common on birch, poplar, maple, beech or oak.

Saprophytic or Parasitic. Indian Pipe (*Monotropa uniflora*) is dependent on an *Armillaria* species, which in turn is connected to the broadleaf tree. Mycelium from these mushrooms may cause the aborted phase of *Entoloma* (page 98). Saprophytic or parasitic.

Young Honey Mushroom buttons

A Honey of an Edible?

Though many eat this mushroom, there needs to be caution in identifying and cooking. There are a number of toxic look-alikes! Also, this mushroom needs thorough cooking, and even then, some people experience stomach upsets.

Deadly Shoestrings

There is more to this *Armillaria* than just edibility. This fungus, unfortunately, is listed as one of the top ten pathogens of trees, especially hardwoods. The fungus produces a root rot called "shoestring rot." Under proper conditions the mushroom spores infect woody shrubs, bases of dead trees or stumps. These serve as a food base from which rhizomorphs are produced. Rhizomorphs are black or red-brown shoestring-like cords of hyphae, about the diameter of a pencil. They can grow through the soil for many feet and when they come into contact with the roots of a susceptible host, they penetrate the bark, moving directly into the cambium and bark tissues. White fans of mycelium develop under the bark. (Both the rhizomorphs and fans can be seen by peeling away the bark of dead tree.) Decay occurs in the woody tissue of roots and base of the infected tree or shrub. Sometimes the process is undetected until the mushroom fruits and its crowd of mushroom caps is seen. Chiefly endangered by this fungus are Northern Red Oak, maples, birches, apples and conifers.

Glow-in-the-Dark Fungus

Under certain conditions (especially following a good rain), mycelium of *Armillaria mellea* may be luminescent in host wood. It glows in the dark creating an eerie light called "foxfire" on the forest floor.

Spore Print

Gills: decurrent and well-separated

World's Largest Living Thing

"**S**tep up and look down ladies and gentleman! See the world's largest living thing!" It's true. A close relative of the Honey Mushroom is reputed to be one of the largest living things ever discovered. In Michigan's Upper Peninsula near Crystal Falls, researchers, using DNA testing and other genetic data, found the interconnected rhizomorphs of a single *Armillaria galica* that were spread through, and underlying some 30 acres of forest. The fungus is estimated to be 1,500 years old.

In the state of Washington, a growth of another immense *Armillaria* (ostoyae) has been discovered, covering about 2.5 square miles of land. A still larger *Armillaria* oystoyae has been discovered and studied in Oregon. Its fungal outline stretches 3.5 miles across and it extends an average of three feet into the ground. It is estimated to have existed over 2,000 years.

Velvet-footed Pax
Paxillus atrotomentosus

A group of these mushrooms is an impressive sight. They emerge sometimes four or five at a time from well-rotted conifer wood. Their sturdiness and large size gives them a bold look. The dry, downy cap of this mushroom varies from yellow to rust brown and becomes darker with age displaying a matting of brown-black wool. It is flat at maturity with in-rolled margin. The flesh of the cap is tough, thick and watery and yellowish-buff in color. Sometimes when you cut the cap, you find a pinkish spotting or marbling in the flesh. The entire top skin, called the cuticle, can easily be pulled away from the cap. The dull yellow gills reach a short way down the stalk. They fork near the stalk and sometimes form into pore-like structures. The gills easily detach from the lower cap surface.

Cap: 1½–6" wide

Most striking is the appearance of the solid, bulky stalk. It is light yellow at the top but most of its surface is covered with a velvety mat of brown–black hairs. The stalk often has an off-center or lateral attachment to the cap.

Stem: 3½–5" tall

Habitat
Alone, scattered or in clusters on well-decayed conifer logs, stumps or buried wood; especially pine. Saprophytic.

Velvet-footed Pax

A Case of Rot
Paxillus atrotomentosus is one of the mushrooms that causes brown rot. If you lift the mushroom from its host base, you will notice that the wood left behind is crumbly, brown and often broken into cube-like pieces. Fungi that cause brown rot are able to digest only the cellulose component of the wood. When the cellulose is destroyed, what remains is the brown lignum.

Dyer's Note
Dye extracted from this fungus can turn yarns a lovely moss-green.

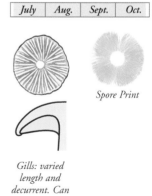

July	Aug.	Sept.	Oct.

Spore Print

Gills: varied length and decurrent. Can form pore-like structures

Velvet Foot
Flammulina velutipes

Tufts of these petite mushrooms with orange caps appear on hardwood stumps. The orange-yellow to burnt-orange cap is smooth, shiny and sticky with a dark center and light margin. The margin is inrolled and faintly lined. Cap flesh is pale yellow. Gills are attached, cream-colored, narrow and close. Long and short gills intermix and gill edges are minutely fringed with fibers. The feature to especially note is the tough, tapering stem made dark and velvety by brown-black hairs. The stem is hollow and may be curved or twisted. The base often has a coating of white mycelium. This is one of the only mushrooms fruiting above ground during the winter. Winter fruiting can be expected if there is sufficient moisture and several consecutive days without freezing temperatures.

Habitat
Found on hardwood stumps, logs, roots, and sometimes on living trees

May	June	July	Aug.	Sept.	Oct.

Enotake (enokitake)
A cultivated form of this mushroom called enotake is sold in Asian specialty stores and in supermarkets. It has long, spaghetti-like stems and tiny caps with little resemblance to the wild Velvet Foot. The mushrooms are packaged in bunches and sold as an unusual addition to salads. They are said to taste like grapes.

Spore Print

Gills: spaced, varied length and attached

Cap: ½–2" wide

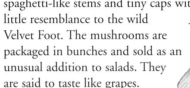

Note
velvety hairs
on base of stem

Velvet
Foot

Stem:
1–3"
tall

GILLED
on
OTHER

Not all gilled fungi sprout from the ground or decaying wood; some sprout from cones, leaves or even other mushrooms. *Baeospora myosura* requires the cones of conifers as a substrate. It is often found on fallen White Pine cones. *Marasmius capillaris* needs fallen oak leaves; it sprouts from the leaf veins. A unique little parasite is the Powder Cap; clusters of cute little white mushrooms stand triumphantly from the tops of defeated rotting masses of old *Lactarius* and *Russula* caps.

Even "Moose marbles" are an acceptable substrate for some gilled fungi; Dung Roundhead fruits from the droppings of Moose, deer, cows and horses. Keep an eye out for this fascinating fungus…and watch out for the dung too!

Powder Cap
Asterophora lycoperdoides (Nyctalis asterophora)

Clusters of these tiny parasitic mushrooms can be found on old *Russulas* and *Lactarius* caps. They resemble a puffball when young; but this parasite has gills. The entire fruiting body starts white, eventually becoming misshapen and densely covered with brown powder. This fascinating fungus parasitizes other mushrooms, often after the host mushroom has been reduced to a blackish, unidentifiable mush. We do know that they often parasitize species in the *Russula nigricans* group.

The white Powder Caps will eventually be covered in a fine brown powder (hence its common name).

Habitat
Clustered on other decaying mushrooms; especially *Lactarius* and *Russula*. May be hard to recognize the host mushroom. Parasitic.

Puffballs? Not!
These small mushrooms may be mistaken for puffballs due to their poorly formed gills and rounded cap; but there are no parasitic puffballs.

The host mushroom is often not this well preserved; it may be just an unrecognizable black mass of mush.

| July | Aug. | Sept. | Oct. | Nov. |

Cap: ⅜–¾" wide

Spore Print

Oak-leaf Marasmius
Marasmius capillaris

A fun find. This delicate mushroom is found on fallen leaves of broadleaf trees, especially oak, during periods of prolonged rain. Each individual emerges from a leaf vein. They sport a deeply grooved umbrella-shaped cap with a tiny central depression. The cap is buff-colored and has a parchment-like texture. The white gills are set far apart. The black, shiny stem is almost as fine as a hair and is wiry and tough. The mushroom appears quickly after rain and disappears quickly as the woods dry out.

Spore Print

Habitat
Deciduous woods. Scattered to gregarious on dead oak leaves. Saprophytic.

Gills: widely spaced, varied length and attached

Each stem arises from a leaf vein; usually on fallen oak leaves after a long wet spell.

The leaf may not be obvious at first: dig through the duff and you'll find it!

Cap: 1/16 – 5/8" wide

Stem: up to 1"

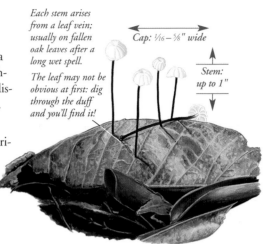

Oak-leaf Marasmius

Cap up to 3/4" wide

Stem: 5/8 – 2"

onifer-
cone
eospora

ok for
tings on
te pine
es after
s of
n.

Sept.	Oct.

Conifer-cone Baeospora
Baeospora myosura

Baeospora myosura inhabits the small world of a single pinecone; often the cone of an Eastern White Pine. The mushroom has a thin, delicate dome-shaped cap with sunken center, smooth moist surface and an inrolled, wavy margin. Cap color is cinnamon or brownish mauve. The narrow white gills are attached and exceptionally crowded. The hollow, spindly stem is initially white but becomes brownish. Its dry surface is covered by minute white hairs and it's often vertically grooved.

Long, loose hairs are found on the stem base. The mushroom is attached to the cone by short white filaments. Best fruiting time is during prolonged wet periods.

Spore Print

Gills: crowded, varied length and attached

Dung Roundhead
Stropharia semiglobata

The shiny, yellow-brown cap of this small dung dweller is usually well rounded (shaped like a half-globe) with a thin, pale, down-turned margin. The cap surface is smooth, hairless and noticeably slimy when wet. It has attached, grayish gills that are very broad with minutely hairy edges. In young specimens they're gray but soon become purple-black as the dark spores are released. The stem is slender, but it's tough, straight and very long. A fragile tissue-like ring may be found on the upper stalk, blackened with falling spores. Sometimes there is little more than a dark fibrous ring zone. Below the ring area, the stalk is exceedingly slimy.

There are a number of other small mushrooms that, like Dung Roundhead, enjoy the comfort and amenities of horse and cow dung. Some are hallucinogenic, some toxic.

Habitat
Paths, fields. Anywhere dung-producing animals produce dung!

Spore Print

Gills: adnate and closely spaced

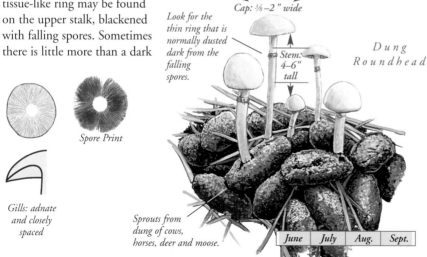

Look for the thin ring that is normally dusted dark from the falling spores.

Cap: ⅜–2 " wide

Stem: 4–6" tall

Dung Roundhead

Sprouts from dung of cows, horses, deer and moose.

| June | July | Aug. | Sept. |

NON-GILLED on GROUND

Don't be fooled by the Boletes. *Boletus, Suillus* and *Leccinum* mushrooms look like your ordinary run-of-the-mill gilled fungi, but a peek beneath the cap will reveal that they lack gills and have about a million holes (pores). These are the tubes from which the spores are released. The unique Hedgehog Mushroom has "teeth" below the cap on which the spores reside.

Morels are also included in this group. In the North Woods, the Black Morel is the most common.

Many other strange fungi are found in this category: the cups, corals, jellies, puffballs and the bizarre Dog Stinkhorn.

Note that some species (several puffballs and bird's-nest species) can be found on both the ground and on very rotted wood.

King Bolete
Boletus edulis

A large, handsome, sturdy-looking mushroom. Its thick cap is broadly rounded to nearly plane with an even margin. The surface is smooth, sometimes slightly wrinkled and feels sticky when wet. Cap color varies widely from yellow-brown, red-brown, biscuit tan, dark red to cinnamon buff. The flesh is firm and white.

Sometimes parasitized by the fungus Sepedonium chrysospermum *which turns the whole body a golden-yellow.*

Cap: 3 ½–10" wide

Stem: 1–10" tall

King Bolete

| June | July | Aug. | Sept. | Oct. |

Look for fine white netting on upper third of stem.

Spore Print

The pore surface starts white, becomes yellowish and, with the release of the spores, turns to olive-yellow. The stem is large in proportion to the cap, very firm, often club-shaped. It's white to ochre in color with red-brown overtones. Look for the presence of fine ridge-like netting (*reticulum*) on the upper third of the stem. Neither cap, spores nor stems stain blue. The mushroom has a pleasant odor.

Habitat
Solitary to scattered on forest floors of conifer (pine and hemlock) and hardwoods (birch and aspen). Often hidden below the duff and leaf layer. Mycorrhizal.

King of Edibles
This choice edible is known worldwide. In Europe, it is the best loved and most sought after of all wild mushrooms.

Slippery Jack (White Pine Bolete)
Suillus americanus

A very common yellow-capped mushroom that is found alone or in large groups in moss and lichen beds in Eastern White Pine stands.

Spore Print

The cap is flat with a low central knob; the margin is decorated by scattered patches of soft red-brown hairs. A flimsy, pale-yellow veil covers young pores, then breaks to form a curtain along the margin rim. The pore surface is a dingy, mustard-yellow, with large angular pores that are elongated radially. They run a short way down the stem.

A spindly, but tough stem supports the cap. The entire surface of the stem is speckled with persistent, sticky, red-brown dots (glandular dots). The stem base is attached to the soil by white or brown cords of mycelium. When you handle this mushroom and its kin, your fingers will stain brown.

July	Aug.	Sept.	Oct.

Habitat
Single to gregarious under Eastern White Pines. Often comes up through dense beds of mosses, lichens or needles. Mycorrhizal.

The slimy/sticky cap has given rise to several colorful common names such as Chicken-fat Suillus and American Slippery Jack.

← 1–4" wide →

Stem: 1⅛–3½" tall

The Boletes

Boletaceae *or* Boletes *are mushrooms characterized by holding their spores in small tubes on the underside of the mushroom, instead of gills. Nearly as widely distributed as gilled mushrooms, they include the famous King Bolete.*

Boletes are a relatively safe group of mushrooms for the table (none are known to be deadly to adults). They are especially suitable for novice mushroom hunters, since there's little danger on confusing them with really dangerous mushrooms, like the poisonous Amanitas. They are easily distinguishable from other fungi by virtue of their pores (and therefore lack of gills), and their thick stems and caps.

Some of the boletes are regarded as culinary delicacies, especially the King Bolete (Boletus edulis). It's generally considered to be one of the tastiest culinary mushrooms found on the forest floor.

Bolete pores

Painted Bolete
Suillus spraguei (Suillus pictus)

An eye catcher! At first glance, this bolete looks as if some artsy person took brush and paint to its cap and stem. The dry, yellow cap surface is overlaid by conspicuous red to dark-red fibrous scales. And the yellow stalk, in harmony with the cap, displays a covering of the same reddish scales. The bolete's cap is rounded, then nearly flat. Its margin is hung with white, cottony veil remnants. The

Cap: 1⅛ – 4½" wide

margin is down-turned initially, but becomes up-lifted and flared as the mushroom matures. Cap flesh is soft, pale yellow, and tends to stain blue or slightly red when bruised.

The yellow pores on the fertile surface are large and angular. They are radially arranged. The yellow stem is solid and may have an enlarged base. A gray, gauzy ring is found on the upper stem. Below the ring, there is a covering of red scales.

Habitat
Scattered or in groups under conifers, especially Eastern White Pine. Mycorrhizal with white pine.

Painted Bolete

Stem: 1⅜–4" tall

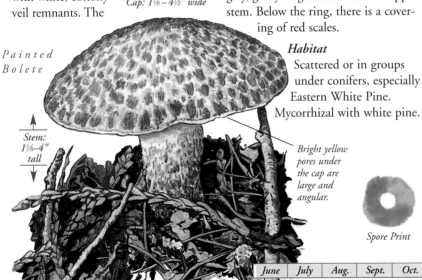

Bright yellow pores under the cap are large and angular.

Spore Print

| June | July | Aug. | Sept. | Oct. |

Blue-staining Bolete
Gyroporus cyanescens

This bolete's blue-staining reaction to injury is so immediate and intense, that you can scratch your name on the pore surface and see it appear in bold-blue. Injury elicits this same prompt bluing reaction from all parts of the mushroom.

G. cyanascens is a sturdy-looking mushroom with a straw-yellow, broadly-rounded cap that becomes depressed and flattened with age. The cap surface is uneven and made coarsely wooly by fibrous scales and mats of hair. The flesh of the cap is thick, rigid and brittle. The fertile underside shows small, round pores and is somewhat sunken around the stem.

Spore Print

The bolete's thick, stout stem is colored like the cap. Its exterior is dry and downy; the interior is stuffed with cottony pith. The stem is often swollen in the middle or at its base.

Habitat
This mushroom is found singly, scattered or in groups or dense clusters on

exposed sandy soil and mosses under second-growth hardwoods or mixed woods; also among rocks. Often along trails and roads. Mycorrhizal.

Blah in appearance—dirty tan in the classic mushroom shape—until you cut it in half. Within seconds the flesh turns a deep inky blue. Color change is very quick.

Cap: 1½–4" wide

Blue-Staining Bolete

Stem: 1½–5" tall

| July | Aug. | Sept. |

Aspen Scaber Stalk
Leccinum insigne

This bolete has a broadly-rounded cinnamon-orange cap with a somewhat grainy or fibrous surface that smooths with age. The margin of the cap over-reaches the pore surface and pieces of the cap cuticle (outer skin) hang down from its rim. The white flesh is thick and soft. Upon injury it stains lilac-gray, then almost black, without any hint of pink or red tints. The pores are a dull yellow. The thick fleshy stem is white and has an enlarged base. Tufts of stiff, brown hairs (scabers) are scattered on the surface. These gradually become black. Stem immediately stains violet to gray-blue when bruised or cut, not red as some look-alikes. The closely related *L. aurantiacum* slooowly turns burgundy or pink when cut or bruised.

Spore Print

Aspen Scaber Stalk

Cap: 1⅝–6" wide

Stem: 3–4½" tall

Pieces of the cap cuticle (outer skin) hang down from its rim.

| June | July | Aug. | Sept. |

Habitat
Scattered or in groups under aspen and birch. May also be under conifers (White Spruce, Jack Pine) in a mixed forest. Mycorrhizal.

Chrome Foot

Tylopilus chromapes (Leccinum chromapes)

Caps are convex to broadly convex, dry, hairy to smooth, pinkish-red to tan. Flesh is white, pink below skin, not staining. Tubes are white to flesh, aging brown. Pores are tiny and round. Stem is white with a pinkish tint and a bright yellow base, and covered with raised reddish dots.

Habitat

Deciduous woods (aspen and birch) and conifer woods (pine and hemlock).

Cap: 1½–6" wide

Cap on fresh specimens dusty rose-colored

Spore Print

Note "scabers" on stalk.

Stem: 2–6" tall

Stalk can be quite variable but the yellow base should be very obvious.

Chrome Foot

June	July	Aug.	Sept.	Oct.

Old Man of the Woods

Strobilomyces floccopus

The dark, densely scaly character of this mushroom makes it hard to spot in the leaf litter and wood debris it inhabits. Large, smoky-black shaggy scales cover the rounded to flat cap. The cap's basic grayish-white flesh shows between the scales. In young specimens, the scales are pyramidal; much like scales on an

Cap: 1–6" wide

Stem: 1½–5" tall

July	Aug.	Sept.	Oct.

Old Man of the Woods

unopened pine cone. The cap margin is hung with a motley array of pallid gray veil remnants. Pores are initially whitish. They are very large and angular. The tough, firm stalk has wooly zones made up of clinging pieces of veil. The portion below these zones is dark and scaly. All parts of the mushroom become reddish, then black, if bruised or cut.

Spore Print

Old and Moldy

The body of this mushroom has a hardiness to it. Dry specimens can be found standing long after spore dispersal. Some remain intact so long that they have a covering of green mold. No wonder the fungus merits the name "Old Man-of-the-Woods."

Habitat

Solitary to scattered in humus and well-rotted wood and leaf clusters among hardwoods (oaks) and conifers (pines). Saprophytic.

Black Morel
Morchella elata

Often the first true morel to appear in spring. Its dark cap is tall and narrowly conical. A network of brown-black ridges divides the surface of the cap vertically and horizontally forming and outlining the deep rectangular, yellow-brown pits (alveoli) where spores will develop. Pits may be irregular due to the path and curves of the ridges. Some longer ridges can be traced from one margin, up over the cap and down to the opposite margin.

Cap and stem are more or less a continuous unit, sometimes showing a crease where cap joins stem. The thick stem is cream-colored to dingy yellow with a surface roughened by a coating of fine granules. The enlarged stem base may be grooved and wrinkled.

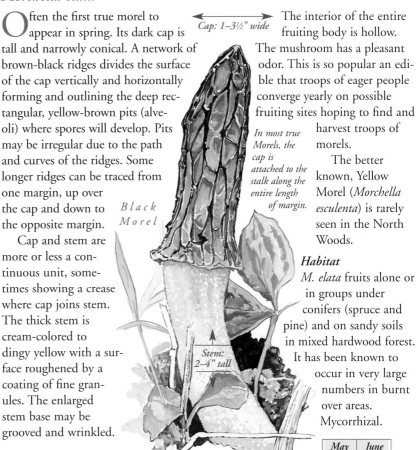

Cap: 1–3½" wide

Black Morel

In most true Morels, the cap is attached to the stalk along the entire length of margin.

Stem: 2–4" tall

The interior of the entire fruiting body is hollow. The mushroom has a pleasant odor. This is so popular an edible that troops of eager people converge yearly on possible fruiting sites hoping to find and harvest troops of morels.

The better known, Yellow Morel (*Morchella esculenta*) is rarely seen in the North Woods.

Habitat

M. elata fruits alone or in groups under conifers (spruce and pine) and on sandy soils in mixed hardwood forest. It has been known to occur in very large numbers in burnt over areas. Mycorrhizal.

| May | June |

Conifer False Morel (Brain Fungus)

Gyromitra esculenta

A very distinctive spring mushroom. The yellow-brown to bay-brown cap of this *Gyromitra* has a convoluted form much like a human brain.

The cap is a complex lobed shape, thin, brittle and waxy. Its interior is hollow and chambered. The thick stem is pallid to buff with a smooth, faintly grooved surface and enlarged base. It has a simple or double chambered interior and, in young specimens, is stuffed with cottony fibrils.

Rocket Fuel Propellant or Tasty Snack?

Controversy swirls around the question of this mushroom's edibility. Many claim to eat and enjoy it without ill effect. However, scientific study of this species has revealed the presence of a carcinogenic toxin, monomethylhydrazine (MMH), used as a propellant for the rocket fuel in the Space Shuttle.

Spore Print

The unpleasant symptoms of MMH occur two to twelve hours after eating, included headache, abdominal pain, cramps, diarrhea and vomiting. In severe cases, liver, kidney and red-cells are damaged. 14 percent of reported poisonings were fatal. But even if you don't get sick at first, the toxins may be cumulative and fatal over time. As mycologist David Arora puts it, "There is a narrow threshold between the amount of MMH the human body can safely absorb and the amount which can cause acute illness, even death. It seems foolhardy to risk eating a mushroom species containing MMH."

Habitat

Solitary or in groups on sandy soil, wood chips, disturbed soil. On ground under balsam, pine, spruce and sometimes aspen. Saprophytic.

May	June

Cap:
2–4" wide, 1–4" high

Stem:
¾–2" tall

Conifer False Morel

Fruiting body is folded and wrinkled like a brain. One of its common names is the Brain Mushroom.

The False Morel's cap is not attached to the stalk except at the very top.

Saddle-shaped False Morel
Gyromitra infula (Helvella infula)

The head of this false morel is typically saddle-shaped. The brittle yellow-brown to red-brown cap has a smooth, undulating surface and a hollow interior. It is not deeply wrinkled or convoluted. Its inward-curving margin is partially attached to the stem and the free margin edges are often very wavy. Two uplifted lobes form twin peaks and create a cleft between them (the "saddle"). Some caps have three lobes and do not form the typical saddle. The stalk is soft and waxy with a smooth, or sometimes velvety surface. It is pallid with hints of pink or yellow. The interior is simple, unchambered and sometimes stuffed with cottony fibrils. Unlike *Helvella crispa* this species is brown with a much smoother, more irregularly lobed stem.

Spore Print

| July | Aug. | Sept. | Oct. |

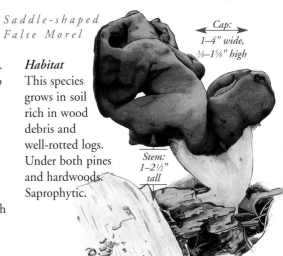

Saddle-shaped False Morel

Cap: 1–4" wide, ⅜–1⅝" high

Stem: 1–2½" tall

Habitat
This species grows in soil rich in wood debris and well-rotted logs. Under both pines and hardwoods. Saprophytic.

Cap: ⅝–2⅜" wide, ⅜–1⅝" high

Stem: 1–3" tall

The cap's underside is densely fuzzy.

White Elfin Saddle

| July | Aug. | Sept. | Oct. |

White Elfin Saddle (White Helvella)
Helvella crispa

Pale coloration and fantastic form give this small mushroom a surreal, cartoon-like aspect. The entire fruiting body is cream-white with hints of yellow or pink. Stem is heavily ridged. The flesh is thin and brittle. When the mushroom emerges, the cap margin is rolled in over the fertile head.

Gradually the margin unrolls becoming quite wildly up-lifted, curved and flared. Some say the mature cap resembles a saddle (hence, the name). The stalk interior is hollow and chambered.

Spore Print

Habitat
Coniferous and deciduous forests. On grass and in the woods.

Black Elfin Saddle
Helvella lacunosa

The coarsely wrinkled cap is gray-brown to dull black. Parts of the cap margin are pressed against, or attached to, the stalk. Other cap lobes arch into double peaks that create a deep, saddle-like cleft. Cup flesh is thin and brittle. The sterile underside is gray-brown to black in color. The dingy white to gray stalk is quite a fantastic work of nature.

Spore Print

The surface is fluted (lacunose); double edged vertical ribs run the length of the stalk and branch irregularly forming pockets and pits. The stem is hollow and chambered. A cross section of its base shows the amazing complexity of the chambering.

Habitat
H. lacunosa is found on the ground in deciduous and coniferous woods.

Black Elfin Saddle

Cap: 1–2" wide, ⅜–2" high

Stem: 2⅝–5" tall

| Aug. | Sept. | Oct. |

Scaly Vase
Gomphus floccosus

Cap: 2–6" wide

Stem: 2–4" tall

Spore Print

Scaly Vase

This mushroom begins as a blunt cylindrical body. It gradually broadens to form a deep, funnel-like or vase-shaped structure. The inner surface is covered with coarse orange to yellow-orange scales. Scales lie flat at the mouth of the funnel, but curl and curve downward over the depressed center. The fertile underside has shallow, rounded wrinkles across its surface. It is pale ochre in color. There is a hollow stem, more or less an extension of the cap, which has cream-buff coloration above and a white base. Fruitings of this fungus appear in groups under conifers or in mixed woods. They sometimes grow in "fairy rings."

Habitat
Solitary, scattered or in groups on soil in conifer or in mixed forests. Saprophytic or mycorrhizal.

| June | July | Aug. | Sept. |

Funnel Polypore (Tiger's Eye)
Coltricia perennis (Polyporus perennis)

This attractive stalked polypore often grows on sandy footpaths in conifer woods. The thin, shallowly depressed cap has a suede-like texture. It is patterned by narrow concentric bands of yellow, gold and varied shades of brown. The margin is typically paler. Cap flesh is rusty brown. Pores are large, angular and slightly decurrent. In mature specimens the pore surface is cinnamon brown. The cap is supported by a sturdy stem that is velvety red-brown. At times, caps of several specimens grow together forming a multi-layered unit.

Habitat
Found sprouting from sandy ground under conifers. Solitary or in groups along paths, roadsides, clearings and edges of burns. Saprophytic.

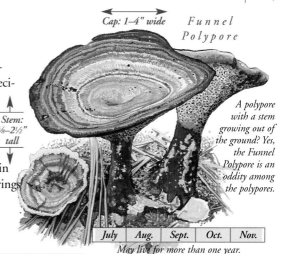

Cap: 1–4" wide

Funnel Polypore

Stem: ⅝–2½" tall

A polypore with a stem growing out of the ground? Yes, the Funnel Polypore is an oddity among the polypores.

| July | Aug. | Sept. | Oct. | Nov. |

May live for more than one year.

Wooly Velvet Polypore
Inonotus tomentosus (Onnia tomentosus)

A polypore with an upper surface that is dry and made velvety by a dense covering of hairs (tomentose). Its yellow-brown cap is circular to fan-shaped with a central depression and lobed, wavy margin. Faint, concentric bands of colors are visible especially near the margin. A vertical cut through the cap reveals 2 layers of flesh; the top layer is soft and pliable, the lower layer fibrous and sturdy. The pores are often angular and in age tear, becoming tooth-like. A dark, rusty-brown stem may be attached centrally or laterally.

Spore Print

Habitat
Fruits on the ground, probably from buried conifer roots and conifer debris. It is also found on the trunks of living and dead conifers, especially pine and spruce. Grows singly or in groups, often with neighboring individual caps fused together at the margins.

Leaves, sticks and needles are often incorporated in the fruiting body.

Cap: 2–6" wide

| Aug. | Sept. | Oct. |

Hedgehog Mushroom
Hydnum repandum

Most common of the toothed mushrooms. Resembles a gilled mushroom from above but a peak below the cap reveals a plethora of spines hanging down like tiny stalactites. The cap is flattish and yellow to brown with a wavy edge.

The Hedgehog bears its spores on the outside of the tooth-like spines, or "teeth."

Cap: 1–4" wide

Habitat
Solitary, scattered or gregarious under mixed woods, often near oaks. Saprophytic or mycorrhizal.

Spines recede as they begin to descend the stem, quickly disappearing.

Stem: 1½–6" tall

Hedgehog Mushroom

Spore Print

| July | Aug. | Sept. | Oct. |

Bleeding Tooth (Strawberries & Cream)
Hydnellum peckii

A strange toothed fungus whose cap surface is velvety and very irregular with pits, ridges and odd horny projections, often incorporating needles. The young cap is white to pink, and when fresh and moist, exudes dark red droplets which cling to the cap surface; this is the "blood" in Bleeding Tooth. As the mushroom matures the cap becomes smoother and is brown to dark red-brown in color. The margin, however, remains white to pinkish and is beaded with red droplets. Flesh of both the cap and stem is leathery to corky with faint zoning of pink-buff, cinnamon-brown, and dark red-brown. The short spines are crowded and

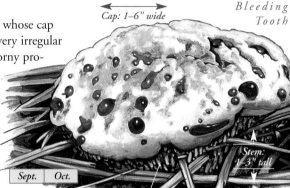

Bleeding Tooth

Cap: 1–6" wide

Stem: 1–3" tall

| Sept. | Oct. |

The "teeth," which are often hidden beneath the irregular cap, extend down the stalk.

usually extend down the stem. They are dull pink, later brownish, with paler tips. The solid stem tapers downward and is rooting. It is colored like the cap and has a felty surface. This mushroom has a fragrant or pungent odor.

The very similar *H. pineticola* has more pinkish droplets and grows under pines.

Habitat
Solitary, scattered or gregarious in fused clusters. On the ground under conifers. Mycorrhizal with pines and spruces in woods.

Spore Print

Common & Green-capped Jelly Babies

Leotia lubrica & Leotia viscosa

Dense clusters of *Leotia* are a fascinating find. Each slimy fruiting body is rather spike-like in appearance with slender, compressed stem and small slightly wrinkly and lobbed. head. They are rubbery and a bit translucent. There are no gills or pores, as the spore development takes place on the surface of the fungus head. Lifting a clump of these small mushrooms brings along sand grains, moss and woody debris

Cap: ½–1½" wide

Stem: ½–2½" tall

Spores are produced on the outer surface of the fungus.

Green-capped Jelly Baby

bound together by strands of mycelium. There are two species commonly encountered. *L. lubrica* is an all yellow-ochre to olive mushroom. The other, *L. viscosa*, differs in having a deep-green head. They are both stuck with the silly moniker, Jelly Baby.

Common Jelly Baby

Cap and stem of new jelly babies are slimy. Stem may be filled with jelly.

Cap: ½–1½" wide

Stem: ½–2½" tall

Habitat

Found in mixed woods, scattered or in groups or clusters (clumps of 50 or more) on soil, duff, leaf litter or mosses, or on very rotten wood. Saprophytic.

July	Aug.	Sept.	Oct.

Jellied False Coral

Tremellodendron pallidum

Coral-like with several or many upright flattened and fused tips. Tougher than true corals, and leathery. Branches are more flattened. Classified as a jelly fungus because of its spores. Unique from other coral fungi in that it has a longish stem and grows on the ground.

Habitat

Solitary, scattered or in groups on ground in mixed or deciduous woods. Saprophytic.

Fungi: 2–4" tall

Jellied False Coral

July	Aug.	Sept.	Oct.	Nov.

Dead Man's Fingers
Xylaria polymorpha

Okay, some fungus names are silly— "Witches Butter" for example—but this one is dead on…excuse the pun. When you see a cluster of gray-black *Xylaria* sprouting from the forest floor visions of **Night of the Living Dead** come to mind: clumps protrude grotesquely from the leaf litter looking like the decomposing fingers of a human hand. Thus, the macabre name, "Dead Man's Fingers."

When young and developing, this fungus looks more like "Dead Man's Nose."

The clubs are rounded at

Spores are produced on miniscule organs that pierce the outer crust of the fungus.

**Fungus:
¾–3¼" tall**

Mushrooms start out more whitish but turn blackish later in the season.

the tip and are supported at the base by a short, cylindrical stalk. Clubs have a very hard, winkled exterior and are often twisted and distorted. The inner flesh is white, fibrous and tough. The club is basically a mass of fungal tissue (*stoma*) that houses flask-like spore-producing organs. The ends of the tiny "flasks" (*perithecia*) pierce the outer skin of the club and give it a pimpled, roughened look. The fungus fruits whitish in spring and by summer takes on a black coloration.

Habitat

Clubs are usually found at soil level attached to below-ground rotting deciduous wood. They tend to grow in clusters on or near rotting wood and stumps of beech, maple, elm, birch or basswood. Saprophytic.

¾" wide

| June | July | Aug. | Sept. | Oct. |

Dead Man's Fingers

Yellow Fairy Fan
Spathularia flavida

It is a delight to find a colony of these small fungi carpeting a patch of pine woods. Their design is whimsical, suggesting a dainty, lady's hand fan. The cream-yellow upper part of the mushroom is flattened and spread in the form of a fan or spatula. Its surface may be smooth or wrinkled and is

Cap: 1¼–1¼" wide

**Fungus:
⅓–4"
tall**

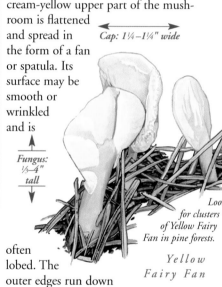

Look for clusters of Yellow Fairy Fan in pine forests.

Yellow Fairy Fan

often lobed. The outer edges run down the stem on opposite sides. The pallid stem is usually tapered upward and threads of white or yellow mycelium are found at the base.

Habitat
Pine forests.

Fungus: 1–4" tall

Strap-shaped Coral

| July | Aug. | Sept. | Oct. |

Strap-shaped Coral
Clavariadelphus ligula

The fruiting body is typically a simple, upright, unbranched club. It is rounded at the top and somewhat flattened or spindle-shaped. The club surface may be smooth, wrinkled or shallowly grooved. It narrows downward to a small, hairy base, which often has mycelial threads holding to the surrounding hummus. The color of the fruiting bodies varies: salmon-buff, brown or yellow-buff. The interior of the club is white and somewhat spongy.

Habitat
This fungus produces large numbers of fruiting bodies scattered or clustered where there is a moist carpeting of pine-needle duff or other woodland debris. Saprophytic.

Purple Club Coral (Purple Tongues)
Clavaria purpurea

The smoky-purple to amethyst color of this delicate club fungus sets it apart from other small clubs. The fruiting body is erect, very slender and tube-like, with rounded or somewhat pointed tip. The outer surface is smooth. The club's interior flesh is white to pale lilac and is quite fragile. With age the club becomes hollow. A whitish, hairy base supports the club.

This fungus fruits in tightly packed clusters or scattered colonies in wet, grassy areas of open woods.

Purple and worm-like but brittle.

Habitat
Groups or clusters (sometimes dense) on wet soil in conifer (spruce and firs) woods. Saprophytic.

| July | Aug. | Sept. | Oct. |

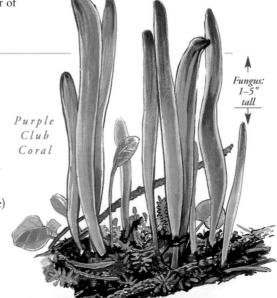

Purple Club Coral

Fungus: 1–5" tall

Yellow Spindle Coral (Golden Fairy Club)
Clavulinopsis laeticolor (Clavulinopsis pulchra)

Scattered stands or tufts of these dainty yellow to golden-orange clubs enliven moist, mossy humus-rich woodlands. The typical club has somewhat flattened sides, a rounded tip and is without branching. The surface is often wrinkled and grooved. The inner flesh is pliant rather than brittle and is whitish or yellow in color. Each club has a stalk-like base that tapers downward. The color fades when the club is dried.

Habitat
Solitary, in groups or clusters on wet and mossy soil in woods. Saprophytic.

| July | Aug. | Sept. | Oct. |

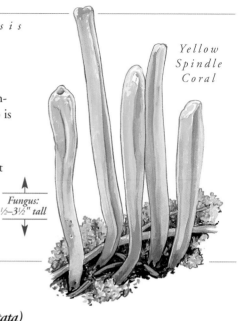

Yellow Spindle Coral

Fungus: ½–3½" tall

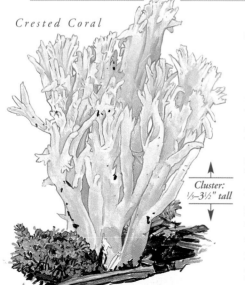

Crested Coral

Cluster: ⅓–3½" tall

Crested Coral
Clavulina cristata (Clavaria cristata)

Delicate, finely toothed (crested) branch tips give a special charm to this small coral. There is a great variety in the form and shape of its fruiting bodies, but usually a slender, white base supports a densely branched structure. The slender branches are irregularly formed; some smooth, some vertically grooved or wrinkled. The upper part of each branch is flattened and the tip decorated with the crest that gives the coral is name, *cristata*. When fresh and young, the coral is pure white to pinkish white. It may become yellowish or gray-ochre in age. A fungal parasite often causes the base of the coral to blacken and the many branches may become flat and fused.

Habitat
Solitary to scattered or densely gregarious on ground in well-shaded woods: hardwoods, conifers, grassy areas. Saprophytic.

| July | Aug. | Sept. | Oct. |

Yellow-tipped Coral
Ramaria formosa

The fruiting body is compact and bush-like, with dense upright branching that rises from a solid, rooting base. The base is white below ground level. The pale branches may be tinted pinkish buff, salmon-pink or orange-pink. The white interior of the branches can be brittle or fibrous. The flesh bruises red-brown then blackens. Flesh is not gelatinous. Form and color of this fungus are in keeping with its name, *formosa* (beautiful).

This is one of a complex of nearly indistinguishable look-alikes.

Habitat
Look for it on humus-rich soils in conifer and hardwood forests. Mycorrhizal.

Note the pinkish-orange stems with yellowish tips. But the pink tinge disappears quickly.

Cluster: 3–6" tall, nearly as wide

Many-branched with "fingers" at tip and no "crowns."

Yellow-tipped Coral

| July | Aug. | Sept. | Oct. |

Dog Stinkhorn
Mutinus caninus

For this strange fungus, life begins in an egg. The egg is oval with a white outer skin and an inner gelatinous layer. The egg splits to free the developing stem-like fruiting body and remains at the base as a sack-shaped volva. The cylindrical headless "stem" that rises from the egg is pink. (The closely related *Mutinus ravenelii* has a white stem.) A slimy olive-brown spore mass covers the upper stem except for the tip. The stem below the spore mass is covered by a network of minute chambers. These chambers capture light, and give the stem an almost crystalline aspect. It is surprisingly beautiful.

It Stinks so Good!
The slime at the tip is foul smelling and sure to offend human sensibilities, but a host of flying and crawling insects find it very attractive and pay a visit, carrying off spores that cling to their feet and bodies, assuring a wide dispersal.

Habitat
Solitary to clustered on ground or rotten wood in gardens, roadsides and woods. Often growing in needle litter, leaf litter, mulch, wood chips, humus, soil, decaying wood in coniferous and deciduous forests. Saprophytic.

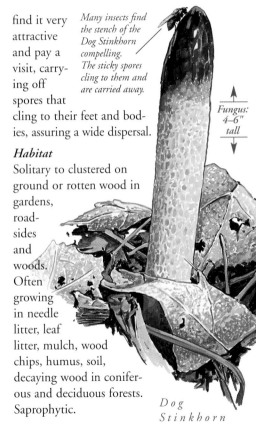

Many insects find the stench of the Dog Stinkhorn compelling. The sticky spores cling to them and are carried away.

Fungus: 4–6" tall

Dog Stinkhorn

| Aug. | Sept. | Oct. |

Pear-shaped Puffball
Lycoperdon pyriforme

The most common puffball. This puffball is nearly round with a narrow, stem-like sterile base. The outer skin (peridium) is white to pale-tan, aging rusty-brown. It is smooth with only a scattering of granules or spines on the top. This outer layer gradually falls off, revealing a smooth inner skin. The upper surface of this surrounding skin will split open in timely fashion to allow release of spores. The spore mass is firm and white at first, then green-yellow and finally, at maturity, olive-brown. The fruiting bodies of this fungus are often found pressed together in large clumps on rotting logs, sawdust and rich organic debris. Old weathered fruiting bodies may be recognizable into the following summer.

A feature of note is the conspicuous massing of white mycelial cords (*rhizomorphs*) that anchor the individual puffball to the wood, connect the puffballs to one another and spread through the host wood or debris bed. This is a good opportunity to get a good look at the rhizomorphs of a fungus.

Size: ½–2"

Young puffball

Mature puffballs: Note split in skin prior to release of spores.

Airborne spores

With Stem: ⅝–1¾" tall

| July | Aug. | Sept. | Oct. | Nov. |

Pear-shaped Puffball

Habitat
Single to dense clusters on rotten logs or stumps, usually decaying deciduous wood, some conifers. Occasionally on ground rich in vegetable fragments. Saprophytic.

The Puffballs

Puffballs are round ground-hugging fungi that could be mistaken for stray golf balls. Most species have a whitish outer husk or shell with spines that slough off after a while. As the densely clustered spores mature inside the puffball into a powdery mass, a pore cracks open at the apex. Any raindrop, deer hoof, hiker's boot or child's poking finger hitting the dried shell will release millions of spores in a tiny cloud that really puts the "puff" in puffball. The wind does the rest.

In young edible puffballs, the spore mass inside is firm and white.

Giant Puffball
Calvatia gigantea

It's a rock, a sleeping sheep, no, it's a Giant Puffball! Well-known and often eaten, this species sometimes reaches enormous size; specimens five feet long and weighing 56 pounds have been reported. Ordinarily though, the fruiting bodies are smaller, perhaps the size of a softball or football. The cream-white spore case is nearly round when young, but flattens and becomes oval as it matures (like a very large lump of dough that awaits kneading). The thick outer skin is smooth and much like kid-leather to the touch. The skin surface eventually cracks into plates of tissue that flake and fall away. An inner, olive-brown layer

8–20" wide

still encloses the spore mass until dispersal. Then, the protective wall disintegrates, exposing the spores (yellow to olive-brown) to the elements.

The Giant Puffball is stemless, but a thick, rooting mycelial cord attaches it to the soil. When white and solid inside, the Giant Puffball is an excellent and eagerly sought-after edible.

Habitat
Solitary or scattered in meadows, fields, gardens, cemeteries, along roads, edge of streams, parks and golf courses. Prefers good rich soil. Saprophytic.

An average-sized specimen has been estimated to hold seven trillion spores.

Giant Puffball

Giant Puffballs are the size of a softball or football but some specimens have reached the enormous proportions of five feet long and 56 pounds!

| July | Aug. | Sept. | Oct. |

Gem-studded Puffball
Lycoperdon perlatum

Dense clusters of these puffballs can be found in open spots along paths, roads and in woodlands. The fruiting body consists of a round top and thick, wrinkled sterile base. The outer wall of the structure is pale-ochre to cream-colored. Its surface is covered by conical spines that add a decorative touch. The spines gradually are shed, leaving networks of open, bare patches across the surface (making it aerolate). The spore mass inside is firm and white, but as the spores mature, it becomes soft and olive-brown. A circular hole develops on top of the fruiting body to release spores for dispersal. It seems a part of the human experience to have put a heel to some of these odd, ball-like entities eliciting an explosive puff of brown powdery dust, blissfully unaware, probably, that you were assisting with the dispersal of countless living spores.

Note cream-white interior—you may be able to eat this one.

Gem-studded Puffball

2–6" wide

1–3" tall

Note the conical spines covering the surface.

Habitat
Clustered in open woods and grasslands. Growing on mulch, compost, humus and woody debris. Saprophytic.

| July | Aug. | Sept. | Oct. |

Pigskin Poison Puffball (Earthball)
Scleroderma citrinum (Scleroderma aurantium)

Very short stalk. Each scale usually has a smaller centered wart with a polygonal background. Ruptures at maturity to form a crater-like opening and exposes the purple-brown spore mass.

Does the specific epithet (*citrinum*) refer to this husk's resemblance to an orange peel? It looks much more like a grapefruit rind. Cut this puffball in half and you will not find the fine white flesh of other species but rather a poisonous mass of purple-black spores. At maturity the shell cracks open irregularly unlike the nice neat pore openings at the tips of other small puffballs.

1-4" wide

1–3" tall

Earthball

Note dark spore body — watch out, it's poisonous!

Habitat
Solitary, scattered or in groups on ground or decaying wood. On or near old stumps in wet spots in conifers and hardwoods. Mycorrhizal with deciduous trees.

| July | Aug. | Sept. | Oct. |

Barometer Earthstar
Astraeus hygrometricus

A small, globe-like structure made up of a thin, papery inner spore sac and tough protective outer skin. The spore sac is whitish, becoming gray-brown with a rough surface. It holds a white spore mass, which eventually, as spores mature, becomes brown and powdery. An irregular opening will develop at the top for spore release.

The unique outer layer splits star-like into blackish-gray rays, each decorated with a distinctive pattern of cracks. The base is attached to the soil by dark mycelial threads. The Earthstar responds to changes in the weather with a surprising bit of acrobatics. In dry weather,

Fungi: 3–4" wide

Barometer Earthstar

the rays close tightly, protectively, around the spore sac. On wet days, the rays spring open, bend back and lift the sac, exposing it to raindrops for an assist with spore dispersal. You can witness the earthstar action by putting closed, dry specimens on a plate and adding water. In a matter of minutes, the stars open and boost the spore sac up on curved rays.

Habitat
Solitary, scattered or in groups in sandy soil, sand dunes, pastures, paths and roadsides. Dry open woodlands. Prefers sandy soils around the Great Lakes.

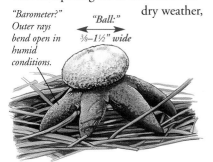

"Barometer?" Outer rays bend open in humid conditions.

"Ball:" ⅜–1½" wide

Sept.	Oct.	Nov.

Body may last all year

Striate Bird's-Nest (Splash Cup)
Cyathus striatus

The cup-like fruiting bodies are noticeable when grouped on dead wood, twigs and woodchips. They look like a bunch of miniature bird nests. A covering of coarse brown hairs gives the outside a shaggy look. Each cup has an inner chamber that is funnel-shaped with shiny, grooved, ochre-gray wall.

At the bottom, are tiny dark packets of spores resembling eggs.

Habitat
Scattered or in groups on dead wood, vegetable debris in open woods; wood chips, twigs, bark, mulch under shrubs. More common during wet times. Saprophytic.

Nest: ⅜" wide

¼–⅝" tall

Striate Bird's-Nest

Gray Bird's-Nest
Cyathus olla

½" wide and deep

"Eggs" are relatively large: up to ½."

Gray Bird's -Nest

The "nest" of this small fungus is actually the fruiting body and the "eggs" are spore packets (peridioles). Outside of the nest is gray to brown and covered with very fine hairs. Inside of nest is smooth gray. The rim of the cup is wavy. It has relatively large eggs. They range from gray to black. At maturity, the top of the nest is ruptured and the eggs expand. Eggs are ejected from the nest by raindrops, due to shape of the nest.

Habitat
May appear in clusters on a well-manured lawn, or on dung. Also found on soil, twigs, wood chips and even on old husks in cornfields.

Fruits July – October.

July	Aug.	Sept.	Oct.

Can be seen all year

Scarlet Cup
Sarcoscypha austriaca (S. coccinea)

Wander about the northern hardwood forests in the spring to search out the stunning Scarlet Cup. When the spring ephemeral flowers begin blooming, Scarlet Cup blazes from the shadows of last year's leaves. Brush away the leaf litter beneath a mature basswood or oak and you may find this treasure. Its fruiting body is a bright scarlet cup, shallow or deeply concave, with an incurved margin.

Spores develop within the cup. The pale underside is frosted by a matting of fine white hairs. The cup sits on a short white stalk.

Native Americans used the cups for medicinal purposes, possible as an antibiotic.

Habitat
Northern hardwood forests. Single or several on rotting branches buried in leaf litter. Saprophytic.

One of the earliest of spring fungi. Usually appears before the trees leaf out. Regularly seen with the spring wildflowers on the forest floor.

Often buried beneath last-years leaves.

| April | May | June |

Cup: 2⅜" wide
1" high

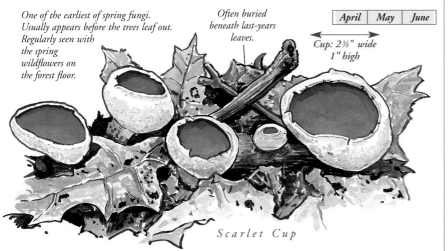

Scarlet Cup

Orange Peel
Aleuria aurantia

A fun fungus with a brilliant orange inner cup (fertile surface) and an outer surface made frosty and paler by a coating of fine white hairs. The cup is very thin and very brittle.

In sunlight it has a translucent quality. Those fruiting bodies, that occur in clusters, become flared and upturned from pressure of neighboring bodies.

⅜–¾" wide

Carrot Color
The orange color of this fungi is chemically similar to carotenoids in plants. Sunlight is required for production of the color.

Orange Peel

Habitat
Scatterings of these orange saucer-like fruiting bodies are found on paths, open woodland soils, and grassy roadsides.

| June | July | Aug. | Sept. | Oct. |

Black Trumpet & Horn of Plenty
Craterellus fallax & Craterellus cornucopioides

You need a sharp eye to spot a *Craterellus*. The dark-brown to black coloration of the trumpet-shaped mushrooms and their uneven, wavy margins camouflage them well in the beds of fallen leaves and woody debris that they like to inhabit. Once you find a group of *Craterellus*, you have an ID choice. There are two almost identical look-alikes: one commonly dubbed Horn of Plenty, the other, Black Trumpet.

The cap is vase-like or trumpet-shaped with an open center that is hollow down to the small brown base that serves as stem. The cap is thin and fragile with wavy, arched margin. The inner surface of the cap is smoky-brown to black. The outer spore-bearing surface may be smooth or wrinkled. Sometimes it is covered by shallow and blunt, vein-like ridges. Color ranges from gray to black.

Habitat
Solitary, scattered or in groups in hardwoods (oaks, beech), hidden in leaves along old roads, trails and open places with mosses. Mycorrhizal.

Fungus: 1–5" tall

⅜–3" wide

Horn of Plenty & Black Trumpet

The mushrooms have a fragrant, pleasant odor suggesting apricot.

Telling them Apart
Craterllus fallax often shows a hint of salmon pink or ochre at the rim of the trumpet and on the outside of the cap (actually a dusting of spores). *Craterellus cornucopioides* lacks any salmon or ochre tints and has a white spore print.

July	Aug.	Sept.	Oct.

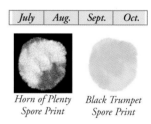

Horn of Plenty Spore Print   *Black Trumpet Spore Print*

NON- GILLED *on* WOOD

Most of us are well acquainted with many of the species in this group. Who hasn't seen an Artist's Bracket fungus? If not in the woods then surely in a gift shop with a woodsy scene etched into the bottom pore surface.

Colorful blobs on rotted logs may be one of the small non-gilled fungi with the equally colorful names: Witches Butter, Eyelash Cup, Lemon Drops or Orange Jelly.

Some of our finest edibles are also in this group. One of the safest is the "Chicken of the Woods" or Sulphur Shelf that grows on oak trunks.

Many folks are curious about the rotting blue wood they find in wet forests. It is the work of Blue Stain, a tiny little cup fungus whose mycelium stains its host wood blue-green.

And if it weren't for the non-gilled-on-wood gang, we would have precious little fungi to admire in winter.

Toothed Jelly
Pseudohydnum gelatinosum

An intriguing little find. A jelly-like fungus that sprouts on very rotted conifer logs. The rubbery fan-shaped cap of this small jelly fungus is translucent, watery-gray, blue gray or brownish and easily overlooked when tucked into the moist mosses on decaying wood where it grows. The cap can be velvety cream to brown and is smooth to slightly downy with thick flexible flesh. The fertile underside is covered by a multitude of tiny soft, translucent spines, looking like miniscule stalactites. A short stem holds

You most definitely need to get on your knees to appreciate this gem of a mushroom. Tiny translucent stalactite-like teeth are packed under the cap. This species is the only toothed jelly fungus.

the cap to the wood. It has the same gelatinous nature and texture as the cap. Sometimes the stem is absent.

Habitat
Solitary, scattered, or gregarious on rotting logs, twigs or stumps, especially hemlock and spruce. Often found on moss-covered logs. Saprophytic.

July	Aug.	Sept.	Oct.

Found on very well-rotted spruce or hemlock logs, often moss covered.

1–3" wide

1–2" tall

Flesh is rubbery.

Toothed Jelly

Note translucence.

Lemon Drops
Bisporella citrina

Hundreds of the fruiting bodies of this cup fungus will create a bright splash of color on hardwood logs. Green moss only accents the bright yellow cups. The tiny, lemon-yellow fruiting bodies have the shape of shallow cups. They are smooth inside and out. The tiny cups taper down to a short, thick stem-like base. Cups may be scattered or densely clustered.

Habitat
In large clusters—maybe in the hundreds—on decaying wood, especially hardwoods: beech, oak, hazel, poplar. On wood lacking bark. Saprophytic.

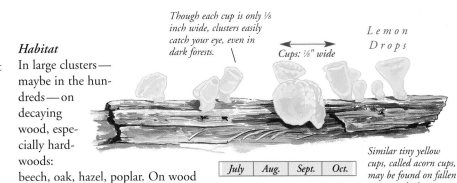

Though each cup is only ⅛ inch wide, clusters easily catch your eye, even in dark forests.

Cups: ⅛" wide

Lemon Drops

July	Aug.	Sept.	Oct.

Similar tiny yellow cups, called acorn cups, may be found on fallen acorns or hickory nuts.

Orange Jelly
Dacrymyces palmatus

Dacrymyces palmatus is a happy little fungus that will brighten any woods walker's day. The orange gelatinous mass occurs on decaying conifer wood. The mass is made up of flattened, irregular lobes of soft, pliable tissue that are arched and convoluted. The jelly mass is attached to the host wood by a tough white rooting base.

The slimy mass eventually deteriorates, releasing the spores.

Butter Buddies
The very similar Witches' Butter (*Tremella mesenterica*) is yellow and fruits on dead hardwood; *Tremella foliacea* is called Brown Witches' Butter.

Habitat
Dense clusters on coniferous logs and stumps; especially spruce. Saprophytic.

Mass: 1–2" wide

The rubbery orange mass of dense lobes fruits on dead conifer branches and stumps. The similar Witches' Butter is more yellow than orange and fruits on dead hardwood.

Orange Jelly

May	June	July	Aug.	Sept.	Oct.	Nov.

Eyelash Cup
Scutellinia setosa

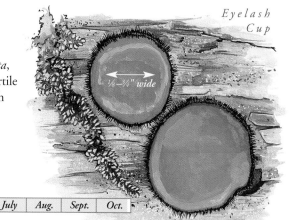

Eyelash Cup

⅛–¾" *wide*

Any fashion model would be so lucky to have eyelashes as fine as this fungus. Black stiff hairs ring every cup. The small fruiting bodies are closed at first, but open out to forms shallow cups. The stalkless cups are pale orange-yellow to dull orange with a smooth fertile surface. The cups appear in clusters on rotted deciduous wood. A related fungus, *S. scutellata*, has a bright vermillion fertile surface and is fringed with black hairs.

Habitat
Mostly in woods; often growing in dense groups with mosses on decaying logs. Saprophytic.

July	Aug.	Sept.	Oct.

Blue Stain (Green Cups)
Chlorociboria aeruginascens

Blue Stain

⅛–⅜" *wide*

You may occasionally come upon a blue-green log or scatterings of blue-tinted wood debris as you walk woodland trails. This unusual coloration is the work of a fungus that produces tiny cup-like fruiting bodies and bears the not tiny name, *Chlorociboria aeruginascens*. It is one of the few fungi known better for its effects on wood than for its fruiting body.

Once established in downed timber, its mycelium branches out and spreads through the wood, exuding, as part of its life processes, a blue-green dye. You are lucky if you find this fungus at fruiting stage with crowds of small brightly-hued caps. The fruiting bodies only emerge after a long wet spell.

Habitat
Mixed woods. Saprophytic.

Fruiting bodies look like tiny cup-shaped growths with stems less than ¼-inch tall

The blue-green-stained wood is evident all year-round

June	July	Aug.	Sept.	Oct.	Nov.

Can be seen on decaying wood year-round.

Brown Cup
Peziza praetervisa

Campers may find this small cup fungus occupying the campsite fire ring as it thrives on the charred wood of earlier fires. The fruiting bodies are globe-like when they emerge, then gradually open to form shallow, stemless cups with wavy rims. The fertile inner lining of the young cup is purple to purple-brown, becoming brown with age. The cups may appear in clusters or as a scattering of individuals.

Habitat
Scattered or in clusters on burnt ground and amongst charred wood in campsites fireplaces. Saprophytic.

Cup Cousins
Several other smooth brown cup fungi may grow here:

Peziza badio-confusa: on ground in woods.

Peziza repanda: on clusters of hardwood logs, humus, wood chips.

Brown Cup

| June | July | Aug. |

Peziza badia: sandy soil, sawdust, under conifers.

Peziza succosa: damp soil in woods.

Devil's Urn
Urnula craterium

What a perfect name for a jet-black cauldron of a fungus. In early spring you may encounter clusters of these urn-shaped fungi protruding from crevices in downed deciduous wood. It is one of the first fungi to fruit in the northern hardwood forests.

The dark-gray or brown fruiting bodies are tough and leather-like. They open up to reveal deep, black-walled cups where spores develop. The upper edges of the urn are typically scalloped or ragged. A thick stem supports the urn. It is dark in color and its base is surrounded by a mass of mycelial hairs.

Habitat
Look for the Devil's Urn on rotting hardwood sticks or rising from wood buried beneath the leaf bed. They often appear to be growing from the ground but gently pull away the moss or leaf litter to find the rotten host wood.

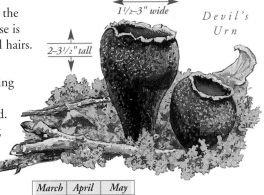

1½–3" wide

2–3½" tall

Devil's Urn

| March | April | May |

Bracket fungi

The following several fungi are bracket fungi, or shelf fungi, and belong to the family Polyporaceae, notable for bearing fruiting bodies (conk) in a "bracket;" several to many individual mushroom caps that lie in a close planar grouping of separate or interwoven horizontal rows. Brackets can range from only a single row of a few caps, to dozens of rows of caps that can weigh several hundred pounds. They are typically tough and sturdy and produce their spores inside the tubes of the undersurface. Many types of bracket fungi are also polypores.

Examples of bracket fungi found in the North Woods include the Artist's Bracket, Sulphur Shelf, Tinder Polypore, Birch Polypore and Turkey Tail.

Birch Polypore

Artist's Bracket
Ganoderma applanatum

This is one fungus that almost every person knows. Large, gray-brown brackets with an uneven crusty surface cling low to large hardwood trees. Individuals may be nearly two feet across! The cap is zoned by a series of deep lines, ridges and furrows. The thin, blunt margin is white. The shelf interior is brown with a corky, woody context and seasonal layers of tubes. Pore surface is white and stains brown if bruised.

You will find many of the shelves covered with the powder of brown spores. Spores are carried from the pores to upper surface of the cap by wind or static charge. This may give spores an advantageous "launching pad."

Shelf Life
A shelf may live and be productive for as long as fifty years!

Perennial, year-round

Habitat
Found on nearly every species of decaying hardwood. It produces white rot in heartwood and sapwood of standing trees.

It's not called "Artist's Bracket" for nothing! Words or pictures scratched into the pore surface stain dark. Intricate designs can be inscribed.

SPARKY LOVES BRIDGET

Artist's Bracket

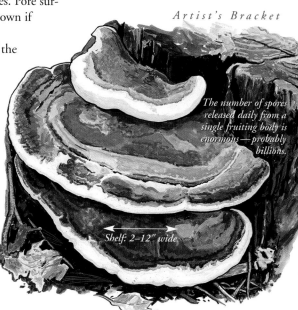

The number of spores released daily from a single fruiting body is enormous — probably billions.

Shelf: 2–12" wide

Lacquered Polypore
Ganoderma lucidum

The upper surface of the semi-circular to circular shelf is covered with a smooth crust, shiny as though lacquered. Color zones move from a central rich dark-red to a band of golden-ochre and then to a cream-yellow at the margin. The zoning is more prominent in some specimens and together with the polished surface, makes them very attractive.

The inner flesh is soft, spongy and white in young shelves, but ages red-brown and becomes woody. Pore surface is cream, becoming yellowish with age. A stalk, if one is present, is thick with a varnished crust like the cap. It is suggested that dried shelves can be broken into pieces and steeped to make a healthful tea.

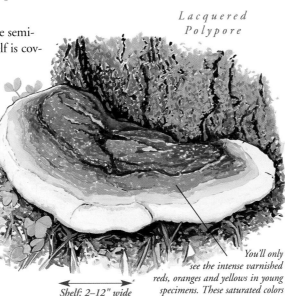

Lacquered Polypore

Shelf: 2–12" wide

You'll only see the intense varnished reds, oranges and yellows in young specimens. These saturated colors will dull to a reddish-brown.

Habitat
Single or clustered on living hardwoods: maples and oaks. May also grow on stumps and roots of some other broadleaf trees. Saprophytic or parasitic.

Year-round

Ling Chi

Forms of G. lucidum *that have a cap AND stem are thought to be the* Ling Chi *written about in ancient Chinese culture. It was documented in Chinese medical texts more than 2000 years ago. Among the 365 species of wood, grasses, herbs, furs, animals and stones utilized by traditional Chinese medicine, Ling Chi was considered of highest value.*

It was called "Herb of Spiritual Potency," or more mundanely "marvelous vegetable." It was said to have many beneficial qualities and was valued particularly to promote the body's resistance to disease. In modern times it's been used in Asia to treat cancer and other diseases. Modern western science has begun to affirm the medicinal potential of elements in G. lucidum *to stimulate the human immune system. Medicinal research has revealed that certain elements can be useful in controlling human conditions; Peptide glycogen can decrease blood sugar and Triperene has shown to decrease blood pressure.*

Hemlock Varnish Shelf
Gandoderma tsugae

A distinctive polypore that is found jutting from hemlock stumps and logs. What you will first notice is that

Like its name implies, the shelf is shiny, appearing to have been varnished.

the cap appears highly polished as though brushed with varnish. It is fan-shaped or irregularly rounded and has an uneven red-brown to maroon surface and a yellowish margin. Often attached to the wood by a sturdy, sometimes twisted, stem that shares the varnished look. Pore surface is white. It stains yellow or brown where injured. Always found on conifer wood.

Habitat
Hemlock and other coniferous forests.

Hemlock Varnish Shelf

Shelf: 2–10" wide

Year-round

Found most readily on Hemlock trunks. When first emerging, it looks like a round knob.

Red-belted Polypore
Fomitopsis pinicola

A striking polypore of decayed conifer stumps and logs, as well as in wounds of living trees. A semi-circular or hoof-shaped shelf with a crusty, resinous, red-brown upper surface and hard, woody interior. The glossy surface is furrowed and ridged concentrically. The cap margin is thick, rounded and creamy yellow. The white pore surface slowly stains yellow when bruised.

Apparently not a picky fungus; F. pinicola has been recorded on more than 100 different species of tree hosts.

Bracket: 2–15" across, 2–8" high

The glossy lacquer-like sheen coating this attractive species will actually melt when a match is held to it.

Red-belted Polypore

Year-round

Habitat
Solitary or in groups on logs and stumps of conifers, especially spruce. Saprophytic on dead trees; parasitic on live conifers and broadleaf trees.

Birch Polypore
Piptoporus betulinus

An old northern woods is certain to have numerous examples of these mushrooms on dying birch, birch snags and logs. The fruiting body of this fungus emerges from the bark as a rounded knob with the look, feel and consistency of a small rubber ball. The cap gradually enlarges into the familiar shelf-like form. The cap is kidney-shaped to broadly rounded, and smoky-brown in color. Cap covering is soft, easily dented and can be readily separated from the underlying white flesh. Young caps are elastic but firm, later the cap becomes hard and corky. The margin is blunt and rounded and projects beyond the pores to form a border. Pores are gray-white and round. With age, the pores dry, crack and become tooth-like. A thick stubby stem attaches the cap to the wood.

Fungus of Many Uses

P. betulinus, being such an abundant species, was noticed by early man and put to good use. It served as a handy fire starter, a razor strop and a "back board" for mounting insect specimens. It was thought to be medicinally beneficial as an antiseptic. The famous prehistoric Ice Man discovered in the Alps had a specimen of this fungus tied to his belt. It was probably carried for its antiseptic qualities.

Habitat

Restricted to trunk or stem of dead birch. Often in damp woods alongside *Fomes fomentarius* (Tinder Polypore). Saprophytic.

Year-round

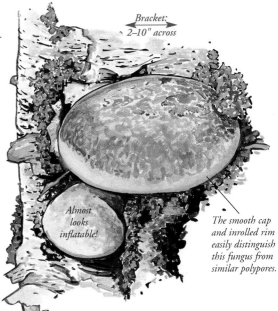

Birch Polypore

Bracket: 2–10" across

Almost looks inflatable!

The smooth cap and inrolled rim easily distinguish this fungus from similar polypores.

Yellow-red Gill Polypore
Gloeophyllum separium

A striking, colorful display of semi-circular or kidney-shaped brackets, clustered, overlapping and often forming rosettes. The tough, stalkless caps are covered with a matting of stiff hairs. Distinct concentric ridges combine with radial wrinkles to create an uneven cap surface. There are bright orange to red-brown color zones with darker tones at the center and a lighter margin.

On the fertile underside, you find a curious maze-like combination of "gill" plates and large elongated pores. The "gills" are radially arranged and are often fused together. (Some specimens may have pores only and the pores sometimes become jagged or tooth-like.)

The maze-like gill structure of Yellow-red Gill Polypore.

Brown Rot
This fungus causes brown rot in both sapwood and heartwood of trees and damages an assortment of structural woods in houses, docks, bridges fences and even telephone poles.

Habitat
May form clusters on dead wood including utility poles, fence posts, boards, bridge timbers, docks, railroad ties, slash and conifer logs and stumps. Hardwoods include birch, hawthorn, poplar, cherry, willow and aspen. Saprophytic

Yellow-red Gill Polypore

Bracket: 1–4" across

June	July	Aug.	Sept.	Oct.	Nov.

Annual to Perennial; may overwinter

Turkey Tail
Trametes versicolor

The name *versicolor*, meaning "variety in color," is a perfect fit for this fungus; no two are colored the same. Its fan-shaped caps range along hardwood logs in overlapping shelves or form rosettes with cap edges joined. They are colorful indeed. Each cap is concentrically zoned with contrasting light and dark colors. These can include cream, beige, blue-green, orange and, many shades of brown. In form and color, the clustered caps resemble the flared tail of a tom turkey. The upper surface of caps has a silken texture and sheen. The margins are thin, waxy and sometimes lobed. The pore surface is white and yellows with age. Pores are very small. This mushroom causes white rot in the wood it inhabits.

Cap: 1–4" wide

May to November
May last several seasons

Turkey Tail

False Turkey Tail (*Stereum ostrea*) is quite similar and may even be found on the same log, but note that its undersides are smooth and lack pores.

Habitat

Dense clusters on dead hardwoods and wounded sites of live trees. May form rows or rosettes on logs and stumps in woods, parks and gardens. Saprophytic.

Papermaking and Turkey Tail

The paper industry employs several wood decaying fungi in the paper making process. T. versicolor is one of them. A major expense in paper making is the removal of brown lignin from wood destined for paper production. Scientists recognized that white rot fungi, with their specialized enzymes, could be a powerful tool in solving the lignum problem. Fungi like T. versicolor are used to chemically alter and bleach pulpwood, chiefly by degrading the lignin components, leaving the desired white wood cellulose.

Dryad's Saddle
Polyporus squamosus

Large flattened, red-brown scales on the cap of this polypore lend it character. The fibrous scales are concentrically arranged on the dry, cream-colored to yellow-brown cap surface. The cap may be circular or fan-shaped with a thin margin. It is often depressed and funnel-like over the stem. The white flesh is soft and succulent in young caps, but becomes corky and tough with age. The fertile surface has wide shallow pores that are irregular and angular. There is a stubby lateral stem darkened at the base by dark brown scales.

Spore Print

Found most commonly in the wounds of living trees especially willows, it is a parasite that causes white rot in the host wood. This mushroom also fruits on a variety of hardwood stumps and logs.

Habitat

Solitary to overlapping clusters. On wounds of living deciduous trees, logs or stumps: elm, maple, willow, poplar and birch in woods, along boulevards or parks. Saprophytic or parasitic.

Cap: 2–12" wide

Dryad's Saddle

May	June	July	Aug.	Sept.	Oct.	Nov.

Sulphur Shelf (Chicken of the Woods)
Laetiporus sulphureus

A shelf fungus like no other; once you find it you won't forget it. A yellow, rubbery knob emerging from the host wood signals the start of fruiting. But that's only a humble prelude to the quick development of multiple overlapping and clustered brackets with bright yellow-orange or salmon tops and intensely yellow undersides. Often, there are enough colorful brackets to occupy the entire side of a living tree trunk or solidly blanket a sizable log.

The caps are flat, semi-circular or fan-shaped with a thick, rounded margin which, in larger brackets, is usually lobed and wavy. The upper surface has suede-like soft matted hairs. The fertile underside of the bracket is bright sulphur-yellow with pores so small they are barely visible without magnification. (Occasionally, a variety is found with a white pore surface.)

This showy mushroom has no dangerous look-alikes and the tender margins of the caps are a choice edible if harvested from hardwood. It has the flavor and consistency of chicken when breaded and sautéed or used as part of a casserole. On the other hand, maybe not; some people have reported allergic reactions to eating and even to handling the mushroom.

One Old Oak
During a recent summer storm, lightning struck a 300-year-old Northern Red Oak that stood on the grounds of a North Woods resort. For several seasons, fruitings of Sulphur Shelf had appeared high up on the oak's trunk, now split and laid open. It was obvious that the fungus had been at work long before the orange and yellow brackets announced its presence; the heartwood was completely decayed and the hollow it left was tightly packed with baton-like masses of mycelium. Had it been spared the lightning strike, the oak might be growing today, still secretly harboring its fungal occupant.

Habitat
This fungus invades and attacks the heartwood of living trees. It causes brown rot that eventually hollows the trunk. Clusters of five to fifty, sometimes forming rosettes, grow on logs, stumps or trunks of deciduous or coniferous trees, especially oaks. May fruit on the same log for several years in a row. Saprophyte.

Note the radial furrowing.

The pale yellow inner flesh is firm but succulent, much softer near the margin and tougher near the point of attachment to the wood.

Sulphur Shelf

Shelf: 2–16" wide

| May | June | July | Aug. | Sept. | Oct. |

Violet Tooth
Trichaptum biforme

This is one of the most common (and most overlooked) polypores in eastern North America. Violet Tooth is not as flashy as its larger cousins. It appears as multiple tiers of petal-shaped or semicircular caps. A bright violet tint can be seen on the cap margin. Caps are tough and flexible and remain leathery even in dry conditions. With age the coloring becomes uniformly white to buff. Pores are mauve in color and become tooth-like and jagged with age.

Habitat
On dead hardwood, especially birch.

½–2 ½" wide

Look for the tiny teeth under the cap.

`Year-round`

Tinder Polypore (Hoof Fungus)
Fomes fomentarius

A very common fungus seen on dead wood and on living trees, especially birch. The perennial brackets are scattered along the wood. In shape, they resemble a horse's hoof. The outer surface of the bracket is thick-crusted and hard. Zones of various shades of gray are set apart by grooves and rounded, wavy ridges. The pore surface is ochre at first then darkens. Pores are round. Each year a new tube/pore layer is developed. This fungus is at pathogen to living trees causing white rot in both the sapwood and heartwood.

The Ice Man Carryeth
Perhaps because the fungus is so widespread and common, men have devised special uses for it. From ancient times it was used as a fire starter; the prehistoric "Ice Man," found frozen in a glacier in the Alps, carried some in his leather pouch. The tube layers (pores) were soaked in saltpeter solution and dried to make a firestarter. It was also hollowed out to carry embers.

In early surgeries it was used as a styptic. The fibers of the upper portion of the bracket were shredded into a soft mass. This was then applied with pressure to a wound, absorbing blood and encourage coagulation.

Fungus: 2–4" tall

Annual growth rings are easily seen.

Up to 4" wide

`Year-round`

Habitat
Solitary or in groups on decaying trees or logs; especially birch and maple, but may also grow on aspen, beech, cherry and poplar. Saprophytic, but may be a parasite on beech and birch, forming white rot.

Northern Tooth (Shelving Tooth)
Climacodon septentrionale (Steccherinum septentrionale)

This large fungus is a woodland oddity. With its many overlapping gray-white caps jutting from a solid backing, it has the look of a misshapen unit of shelving. It resembles a polypore. The caps are sturdy with hairy, uneven upper surface. Each cap is fitted with its own set of fungal dentures in the form of a tight crowd of short pale tooth-like spines that fill the cap underside. Though definitely unappetizing, it's been said that an older specimen, when dried, smells like ham. Yellowish-white when young, becoming tan with age.

Habitat
Fairly high up on Sugar Maples, sometimes beech.

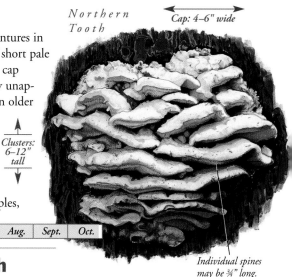

Northern Tooth

Cap: 4–6" wide

Clusters: 6–12" tall

Individual spines may be ¾" long.

July	Aug.	Sept.	Oct.

Bear's Head Tooth

6–12" wide

8–16" tall

Aug.	Sept.	Oct.

Bear's Head Tooth
Hericium americanum (Hericium coralloides)

A thick supporting stem produces many stout, white, fertile branches. These branches divide repeatedly so that a firm compact structure is formed. Each branch tip has tufts or clusters of long, white hanging spines. These create a unique cascading effect or, as some see it, a likeness to the many-layered fur on a bear's head.

Habitat
Look for this unusual mushroom on the sides of hardwood stumps and logs, sometimes on wounds of living trees: maple, beech, oak and hickory. Saprophytic.

Fish-flavored Fungus?
One of the finest, most delectable wild edibles in the North Woods. Sauteed thoroughly it is said to have a flavor reminiscent of fish. The real dilemma is whether to pick this beauty or leave it for other trekkers to enjoy.

Comb Tooth
Hericium coralloides (Hericium ramosum)

An exquisite, pure white fruiting body made up of long, curved branches that rise from a firm, rooting base. Branches fork and produce side branches to form a delicate airy structure. Branches are ornamented by tiny hanging spines arranged, comb-like, in rows along the entire lower surface of branch. Tufts of spines hang from the branch tips. The entire body of the mushroom, aside from the tougher stem, is soft and brittle and has a pleasant odor.

Toothsome Treat
A delicious edible with no poisonous look-alikes. Cook it slowly!

Habitat
The mushroom is found on decaying hardwood trunks, branches and logs, especially birch, maple and beech. It is sometimes hidden out of sight behind loose bark on snags. Saprophytic.

This is a detail of the spines. Like the Bear's Head Tooth *on the previous page, the whole fruitbody is quite large: 4–10" across and 4–6" high.*

Comb Tooth

July	Aug.	Sept.	Oct.

Name Game
The names of the Hericiums (ramosum, corralloides *and* americanus) *are still being shifted about, with various experts and authors applying names to different described species. All the ordinary mushroom hunter can do is look well at the specimen in hand, note its particular features, find the proper description and be aware that guides and texts may differ as to which of the three names is used.*

Crown-tipped Coral
Clavicorona pyxidata

A delicate member of the corals. Its fruiting body has multiple branches rising from a short, felty sterile base. The branches are attractively arranged in tiers with upper branches springing from the enlarged tips of lower branches (a candelabra-like effect). Tips of the outer branches are unique, each with a ring and small branchlets that together form a tiny crown. The body of the coral is pale yellow when young, but darkens and becomes brownish with age, especially in the lower branches.

Crown-tipped Coral

Habitat
This is one of the few corals that fruits on wood. It can be found on well-decayed hardwood stumps and logs; mostly on logs of aspen, willow or birch. Saprophytic.

Clusters: 2–5" tall

June	July	Aug.	Sept.

NON-GILLED *on* OTHER

As in the Gilled-on-Other category, we have several parasitic species that mutate their hosts into completely new forms: "The Lobster" (named for its bright orange skin) and the Aborted Entoloma. They are quite common in the North Woods.

Many folks have encountered the crusty fungus called Black Knot in the woods, but few know what to make of it. Technically it could have been included with the Non-gilled on Wood fungi but it is only found on the young twigs and branches of cherry trees, especially Chokecherry.

The tiny Pine Cone Fungus looks like a gilled mushroom but has teeth under the cap instead of gills. Look for it sprouting from downed pine and spruce cones

Pine Cone Fungus
Auriscalpium vulgare

A. vulgare are easy to identify; you'll find these tiny mushrooms sprouting from pine cones and they're a tooth fungus with a myriad of tiny spines, or "teeth," lining their undersides. They have a fuzzy stalk and the cap is attached laterally, not centered. Late fall specimens may be more mis-shapen than earlier ones.

Cap: ⅜–1½" wide

Stem: 1–3" tall

Habitat
Solitary or in small groups on decaying pine and maybe spruce cones. Also in needle litter, branches and cones of mature conifer woods. They have been found on corncobs. Saprophytic.

| Aug. | Sept. | Oct. |

Spore Print

Black Knot
Apiosporina morbosa

These odd fruiting bodies are knot-like, black growths that clasp and girdle the twigs and small branches of living cherry and plum trees. They are a damaging parasite. The fungus begins as an olive-brown swelling and soon enlarges, ruptures and becomes blackened. During its two-year life cycle it elongates along the branch and encircles it. The fungal growth interferes with the transmission of water and minerals and inhibits transfer of food produced by the leaves to other parts of the tree. The infected branches die and the tree is greatly weakened. In the second year, in early spring after rains, what is called a "shuck slit" occurs, opening the crust to release black fungal spores.

Habitat
Anywhere cherry trees live. Solitary.

Pine Cone Fungus

several or hundreds on a single tree, clasping and enveloping branches. Grows on living cherry trees; especially Chokecherry. Parasitic.

Oozing Food

It is a fascinating fact, that the oozings of these ugly Black Knot fungal masses provide nutrition to a variety of feeding birds and insects.

Year-round

Surface is hard and carbonaceous, but flesh is white when young.

Black Knot

Mycelia embedded in the tree, often causes the affected branches to bend at the site of infection.

Lobster Mushroom
Hypomyces lactifluorum

"The Lobster" is a curious phenomenon. A large, robust, white mushroom is overpowered and transformed by an orange parasite that seems to have less bodily substance than a coat of paint. This parasite constructs a crust-like mycelial cover that gradually engulfs the cap, gills and stem of the host mushroom, leaving only a hint of cap and faint ridges suggesting gills.

The gaudy orange crust holds thousands of tiny spore-producing bodies that appear as pimples on the surface and will eventually open to release spores. This parasite also changes the texture and make-up

Size: Usually 4–6" Varies with host

of entire host body. Large fleshy *Lactarius* and *Russula* mushrooms are its prime targets.

Habitat

Typically, the "Lobster" (parasite-covered mushroom) is found along pathways partially protruding from the soil, with humus and other debris clinging to its surface. Solitary or scattered on ground under conifers and hardwoods.

Lobster Mushroom

| July | Aug. | Sept. | Oct. |

Aborted Entoloma
Entoloma abortivum

The aborted forms are rounded, lumpy white fruiting bodies. Some of them, fanciful observers say, are shaped like pig snouts. Inside, the white flesh is moist and soft. A pink marbling can be seen.

Habitat
Several or in large groups in much-decayed or buried wood, around stumps or rotten woods, decaying logs; under hardwoods. Saprophytic.

Honey, I Aborted the Mushroom!
A strange kind of fungal combat is responsible for producing these odd whitish masses, the aborted mushroom forms found in humus near rotting stumps. One combatant is the small, all-gray mushroom with pink spore print called *Entoloma abortivum*. The other is the Honey Mushroom, *Armillaria mellea*. Just now scientists are pondering the relationship of the two. For years it was thought that the lumpy, soft masses of tissue were ill-formed *E. abortivum* infected by the Honey. Lately, it has been seen the other way around. The aborted forms are thought to be Honeys infected by *E. abortivum*. May the best researcher win.

Spore Print

Aborted form:
1–4" across

Aborted Entoloma

1–2" tall

Entoloma abortivum, *before being attacked by the Honey Mushroom.*

| Aug. | Sept. | Oct. |

SLIME MOLDS

Slime Molds are not fungi, but often share their habitat and are seen in their company. Slime molds lead a hidden life for the most part. They exist as amoeba-like life forms called plasmodiums. They achieve locomotion by oozing through their habitat (soil, wood debris or other organic material) consuming bacteria or microscopic food particles as they go.

At fruiting time, the plasmodium moves to an exposed surface where wind and rain will help with spore dispersal. Once in place, the slime mold plasmodium undergoes metamorphosis.

In accord with its species, the slime mold may form into troops of upright structures resembling miniature brush bristles; it may form a blanket of white or gaudy colored material on stumps, forest debris or on soil; it may form small pea-shaped cushions on logs; or construct other forms, sometimes of fantastic design.

Blackberry Slime
Metatrichia vesparum

This dark, reddish-black slime sheeting rotten wood gives rise to stalks bearing a group of tiny, oval, lidded fruiting bodies (sporangia). The bodies are maroon to black with a metallic shine. The lids are dome-shaped. Their brick-red supporting stalk is fairly thick and

Sporangia

Stem: 1/16–1/8" tall

The clusters arise from a single stalk.

solid and is surrounded at the base by vein-like strands of tissue. Eventually, the lids of the sporangia break open revealing a purplish-red mass, a mix of red threads (capillitium) and spores. Action of the threads helps expedite the release of the mature spores.

Habitat
Found on well-rotted wood.

Head: 1/16" wide

The blue-black sheen of the clustered fruitbodies (sporangia) reminds one of blackberry bunches.

Blackberry Slime

| July | Aug. | Sept. | Oct. |

Chocolate Tube Slime
Stemonitis species

A shining base sheet gives rise to multiple fruiting bodies with elongated, cylindrical tops and short polished black stems. These sporangia form closely-packed erect clusters on a common base. They look like tufts of miniature brush bristles as they range here and there along the host wood. The purple black spores break out of the cylinders at maturity.

Habitat
Dead wood, downed logs in woods.

Comments
Common name refers to the stalked spore-bearing cases. The plasmodium stage is a white mass.

Cap: ¹⁄₃₂ - ¹⁄₁₆ " wide

These cylindrical brown structures are the sporangia.

Stem: ¹⁄₈ - ¹⁄₄ " tall

Wonderful common names for this fungus include Chocolate Tube Slime and Pipecleaner slime. How about "Fudgecicle Slime?"

Chocolate Tube Slime

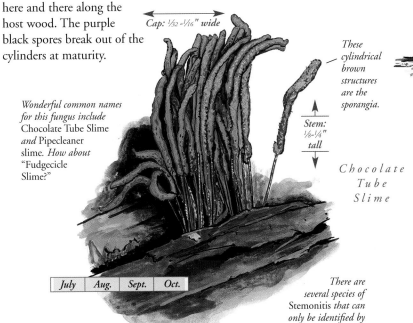

July	Aug.	Sept.	Oct.

There are several species of Stemonitis that can only be identified by microscopic structures.

Red Raspberry Slime
Tubifera ferruginosa

A slime that will stop you in your tracks. When young, these sporangia are beautiful. They are bright rose-red, almost iridescent, and standing in a cluster, may resemble a multi-petaled flower head.

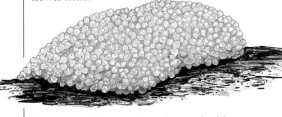

Some groupings press into large cake-like formations. The transparent slime base produces tight crowds of cylindrical to oval fruiting bodies. As the sporangia mature, they leave beauty behind and become a dull purple-brown. The spore mass inside is yellow-brown. Also known as Pink Slime or Rose-red Slime.

Habitat
This slime mold is found on well-rotted logs or leaf litter, often with mosses.

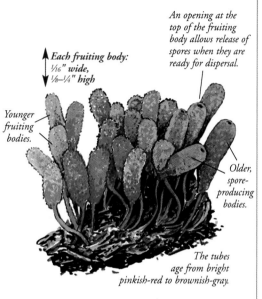

Each fruiting body: 1/16" wide, 1/8–1/4" high

An opening at the top of the fruiting body allows release of spores when they are ready for dispersal.

Younger fruiting bodies.

Older, spore-producing bodies.

The tubes age from bright pinkish-red to brownish-gray.

Red Raspberry Slime

June	July	Aug.	Sept.	Oct.	Nov.

Tapioca Slime
Brefeldia maxima

One of the largest of the slime molds. It spreads widely over the host forming a shiny, silver base for its cushion-like groups of sporangia. The mound of young fruiting bodies is white to off-white and has the look of a spill of thick tapioca pudding. As the sporangial mass matures, it becomes pink tinged and finally purple-brown and crust-like. Brownish-purple black spores are released when the outer crust crumbles and breaks away. Found on dead wood and living plants.

Habitat
May fruit on living or dead wood.

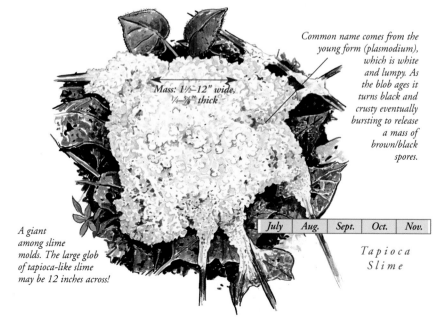

Mass: 1½–12" wide, ¼–⅜" thick

Common name comes from the young form (plasmodium), which is white and lumpy. As the blob ages it turns black and crusty eventually bursting to release a mass of brown/black spores.

A giant among slime molds. The large glob of tapioca-like slime may be 12 inches across!

July	Aug.	Sept.	Oct.	Nov.

Tapioca Slime

FUNGUS CHECKLIST

GILLED ON GROUND
- ❏ Fly Amanita
- ❏ Destroying Angel
- ❏ Tawny Grisette
- ❏ Yellow Swamp Russula
- ❏ Emetic Russula
- ❏ Short-stalked White Russula
- ❏ Rooted Collybia
- ❏ Chanterelle
- ❏ False Chanterelle
- ❏ Forest Funnel Cap
- ❏ The Miller
- ❏ Wine Cap Stropharia
- ❏ Saffron Milk Cap
- ❏ Indigo Milk Cap
- ❏ Pepper Milk Cap
- ❏ Violet (Purple) Cort
- ❏ Spotted Cort
- ❏ Rimmed-Bulb Cort
- ❏ Red-gilled Cort
- ❏ Witch's Hat
- ❏ Scarlet Waxy Cap
- ❏ White or Ivory Waxy Cap
- ❏ Parrot Waxy Cap
- ❏ Alcohol Inky
- ❏ Shaggy Mane
- ❏ Meadow Mushroom
- ❏ Shaggy Parasol
- ❏ Blewit

GILLED ON WOOD
- ❏ Bleeding Fairy Helmet
- ❏ Pinwheel Marasmius
- ❏ Fuzzy Foot
- ❏ Jack O' Lantern
- ❏ Sharp-scaly Pholiota
- ❏ Scaly Pholiota
- ❏ Crinkle Gill
- ❏ Split Gill
- ❏ Oyster Mushroom
- ❏ Netted Rhodotus
- ❏ Tree Volvariella
- ❏ Deer Mushroom
- ❏ Clustered Collybia
- ❏ Platterfull Mushroom
- ❏ Honey Mushroom
- ❏ Velvet-footed Pax
- ❏ Velvet Foot

GILLED ON OTHER
- ❏ Powder Cap
- ❏ Oak-leaf Marasmius
- ❏ Conifer-cone Baeospora
- ❏ Dung Roundhead

NON-GILLED ON GROUND
- ❏ King Bolete
- ❏ Slippery Jack (White Pine Bolete)
- ❏ Painted Bolete
- ❏ Blue-staining Bolete
- ❏ Aspen Scaber Stalk
- ❏ Chrome Foot
- ❏ Old Man of the Woods
- ❏ Black Morel
- ❏ Conifer False Morel
- ❏ Saddle-shaped False Morel
- ❏ White Elfin Saddle
- ❏ Black Elfin Saddle
- ❏ Scaly Vase
- ❏ Funnel Polypore (Tiger's Eye)
- ❏ Wooly Velvet Polypore
- ❏ Hedgehog Mushroom
- ❏ Bleeding Tooth
- ❏ Green-capped Jelly Baby
- ❏ Common Jelly Baby
- ❏ Jellied False Coral
- ❏ Dead Man's Fingers
- ❏ Yellow Fairy Fan
- ❏ Strap-shaped Coral
- ❏ Purple Club Coral
- ❏ Yellow Spindle Coral
- ❏ Crested Coral
- ❏ Yellow-tipped Coral
- ❏ Dog Stinkhorn
- ❏ Pear-shaped Puffball
- ❏ Giant Puffball
- ❏ Gem-studded Puffball
- ❏ Pigskin Poison Puffball (Earthball)
- ❏ Barometer Earthstar
- ❏ Gray Bird's-Nest
- ❏ Striate Bird's-Nest (Splash Cup)

- ❑ *Scarlet Cup*
- ❑ *Orange Peel*
- ❑ *Black Trumpet*
- ❑ *Horn of Plenty*

NON-GILLED ON WOOD
- ❑ *Toothed Jelly*
- ❑ *Lemon Drops*
- ❑ *Orange Jelly*
- ❑ *Witch's Butter*
- ❑ *Eyelash Cup*
- ❑ *Blue Stain (Green Cups)*
- ❑ *Brown Cup*
- ❑ *Devil's Urn*
- ❑ *Artist's Bracket*
- ❑ *Lacquered Polypore*
- ❑ *Hemlock Varnish Shelf*
- ❑ *Red-belted Polypore*
- ❑ *Birch Polypore*
- ❑ *Yellow-red Gill Polypore*
- ❑ *Turkey Tail*
- ❑ *Dryad's Saddle*
- ❑ *Sulphur Shelf (Chicken of the Woods)*
- ❑ *Violet Tooth*
- ❑ *Tinder Polypore*
- ❑ *Northern Tooth*
- ❑ *Bear's Head Tooth*
- ❑ *Comb Tooth*
- ❑ *Crown-tipped Coral*

NON-GILLED ON OTHER
- ❑ *Pine Cone Fungus*
- ❑ *Black Knot*
- ❑ *Lobster Mushroom*
- ❑ *Aborted Entoloma*

SLIME MOLDS
- ❑ *Blackberry Slime*
- ❑ *Chocolate Tube Slime*
- ❑ *Tapioca Slime*
- ❑ *Red Raspberry Slime*

TITLES OF INTEREST

Arora, D. 1986. *Mushrooms Demystified.* Berkley, CA: Ten Speed Press.

Barron, G. 1999. *Mushrooms of Northeast North America.* Edmonton, AB: Lone Pine Press.

Bessette, A. 1995. *Mushrooms of North America in Color.* Syracuse, NY: Syracuse University.

Bessette, A., A. R. and D. W. Fischer. 1997. *Mushrooms of Northeastern North America.* Syracuse, NY: Syracuse University.

Bossenmaier, E. F. 1997. *Mushrooms of the Boreal Forest.* Saskatoon, SK: University of Saskatchewan.

Farr, M. 1981. *How to Know the True Slime Molds.* Dubuque, IA: Wm. C. Brown.

Glick, P. G. 1979. *The Mushroom Trailguide.* New York, NY: Holt, Rinehart and Winston.

Graham, V. O. 1944. *Mushrooms of the Great Lakes.* New York, NY: Dover.

Hudler, G. W. 1998. *Magical Mushrooms, Mischievous Molds.* Princeton, NJ: Princeton University Press.

Kauffman, C.H. 1971. *Gilled Mushrooms of Michigan and the Great Lakes Region, 2 vols.* New York, NY: Dover Publications.

Kendrick, B. 1992. *The Fifth Kingdom.* Waterloo, IA: University of Waterloo.

Laessoe, T. 1996. *The Mushroom Book.* New York, NY: DK Publishing.

Laessoe, T., and G. Lincoff. 2002. *Smithsonian Handbooks: Mushrooms.* New York, NY: DK Publishing.

Lincoff, G. 1984. *The Audubon Society Field Guide to North American Mushrooms.* New York, NY: Knopf.

McKnight, K. H., and V. B. McKnight. 1987. *A Field Guide to Mushrooms of North American.* New York, NY: Houghton Mifflin.

McIlvaine, C., and R. K. Macadam. 1973. *One Thousand American Fungi.* New York, NY: Dover Publications.

Miller Jr., O. K., and H. H. Miller. 2006. *North American Mushrooms.* Gilford, CT: Falcon Guide.

Phillips, R. 2005. *Mushrooms and other Fungi of North America.* Buffalo, NY: Firefly Books.

Schaechter, E. 1998. *In the Company of Mushrooms.* Cambridge, MA: Harvard University Press.

Smith, A. H. 1980. *The Mushroom Hunter's Field Guide.* Ann Arbor, MI: University of Michigan Press.

Smith, A. H. 1981. *How to Know Non-Gilled Mushrooms.* New York, NY: Wm. Brown.

Smith, A. H., H. V. Smith and N. Weber. 1979. *How to Know the Gilled Mushrooms.* Dubuque, IA: Wm. C. Brown.

Tekeila, S. 1993. *Start Mushrooming.* Cambridge, MN: Adventure Publications.

GLOSSARY

adnate: Gills attached to the stalk without a notch.

adnexed: Gills attached to the stalk with a notch.

annular Zone: A poorly defined ring on the stalk.

annulus: A ring on the stalk.

apex: The uppermost portion of the stalk.

apendiculate: With pieces of the veil hanging along the margin.

ascomycetes: A major group of fungi that includes those species that produce ascospores in asci (sacs).

ascospore: Spore formed within an ascus (sac).

ascus: A sac-like structure where the ascospores are formed. (*asci*: plural)

asexual: Cells are body parts not resulting from fertilization.

attached: Gills joined to the stalk.

basal: Located at the base of a structure such as a stalk.

basidiomycetes: A major group of fungi that includes those species that produce spores borne on a basidium.

basidiospore: A spore formed on a basidium.

basidium: A club-shaped structure where the spores are formed in. (*basidia*: plural)

basidiomycetes: Such as gilled mushrooms.

bracket: Shelflike fruiting body produced by wood-rotting basidiomycetes.

bruising: Changing color when handled.

button: The immature stage of a mushroom.

clavate: Club-shaped.

coniferous: Cone-bearing.

conk: A large, woody, hoof-shaped polypore growing on wood.

corrugated: Wrinkled, usually with long wavelike ridges.

cortina: Spiderweb-like growth from stalk to cap.

crenate: With uniform rounded lobes; refers to margin of cap.

cristate: Fine branching tips as in some coral fungi.

cup: The saclike tissue at the stalk base left by the universal veil after it has ruptured of some mushrooms.

cuticle: The outermost tissue layer of the cap; skin.

decurrent: Gills that descend or run down the stalk.

deliquesce: Liquify; as in the gills of the genus Coprinus.

disc: The central area of the surface of a mushroom cap.

duff: The partially decayed plant material on the forest floor.

egg: The immature button stage of amanitas and stinkhorns.

fairy Ring: An arc or circle of gilled mushrooms or puffballs arising from a mycelium that expands outward from a central point.

fibril: A tiny fiber.

filiform: Thread-like.

flesh: The inner tissue of a fruiting body.

fluted: Having sharp-cornered ridges extending down the stalk.

free: Gills that are not attached to the stalk.

fruiting body: The fleshy to hard reproductive structure of a fungus, commonly called a mushroom.

GLOSSARY

fusiform: Spindle-shaped; tapering at both ends.

gasteromycetes: A group of Basidiomycetes, such as puffballs, which produce spores in closed chambers within the fruiting body.

glabrous: Bald and smooth.

gleba: Spore-bearing tissue of stinkhorns.

globose: Round; globe-like.

gregarious: Closely scattered over a small area.

heartwood: The inner, usually dead wood, of a tree trunk.

hirsute: Covered with a dense layer of long stiff hairs.

humus: Partially decomposed plant material.

hypha (hyphae): Thread-like filaments of fungi.

inner veil: Another name for partial veil.

lamella: A gill on the underside of the cap of a mushroom.

latex: A watery or milk-like fluid that exudes from some mushrooms when they are cut or bruised.

lignicolous: Growing on wood.

lubricous: Smooth and slippery.

mycelium: A mass of hyphae, typically hidden in a substrate.

mycology: The scientific study of fungi.

mycorrhizal: Having a mutually beneficial relationship with a tree or other plant.

myxomycota: Division of fungi containing the slime molds.

ovate: Shaped like an egg.

ovoid: Somewhat egg-shaped.

parasite: An organism that obtains its nutrients from a living host.

partial veil: A layer of fungal tissue that covers the gills or pores (under the cap) of some immature mushrooms.

pedicels: Slender stalks.

pileus: The cap of the mushroom fruiting body.

piriform: Pear-shaped.

plasmodium: The vegetative stage of a slime mold.

plicate: Deeply grooved, sometimes pleated or folded.

pores: The open ends of the tubes of a bolete or polypore.

pore surface: The undersurface of the cap of a bolete or polypore, where the open ends of the tubes are visible.

pubescent: Having short, soft, downy hairs.

punctate: Marked with tiny points, dots, scales or spots.

putrescent: Soon decaying.

radial: Pointed away from a common central point, like the spokes of a wheel.

recurved: Curved backward or downward.

reticulate: Covered with a net-like pattern of ridges.

rhizomorph: A group of thick, rope-like strands of hyphae growing together as a single organized unit.

rimose: Having distinct cracks or crevices.

ring: Remnants of a partial veil that remain attached to the stalk after the veil ruptures.

saccate: Sheath-like or cup-shaped.

saprophyte: An organism that lives off dead or decaying matter.

sapwood: The living, outer layer of a tree trunk.

scabers: Small, stiff, granular points on the surface of the stalks of some mushrooms.

scabrous: Rough, with short rigid projections.

scale: An erect, flattened, or recurved projection or torn portion of the cap or stalk surface.

sessile: Fruiting bodies that lack a stalk.

setaceous: Stalk with bristles.

serrate: Jagged or toothed like a saw blade.

sexual: Pertaining to fertilization involving two compatible cells.

shelflike (stalkless): Typically growing from wood; usually horizontal, like a shelf.

sinuate: Gills that gradually narrow and become concave near the stalk.

spathulate: Spoon-shaped.

spines: Tapered, downward-pointing projections on the undersurface of some mushroom caps.

sporangium: A sac-like microscopic structure in which asexual spores are produced.

spore: A microscopic reproductive cell with the ability to germinate and form hyphae.

spore case: A structure containing the spore mass in species of Gasteromycetes.

squamose: Having scales.

stalk: The structure that arises from the substrate and supports the cap or spore case of a mushroom; also called stem or stipe.

stellate: Starlike.

stipe: The stalk or stem that supports a mushroom.

striate: Having small, more or less parallel lines or furrows.

strigose: Coated with long, coarse, stiff hairs.

sulcate: Grooved.

subdecurrant: Gills extending slightly down the stalk.

substrate: Organic matter that serves as a food source for a fungal mycelium.

superficial: Merely resting on the surface; not attached.

superior ring: A ring located on the upper stalk surface.

symbiont: An organism that lives in a mutually beneficial relationship, or symbiosis, with another organism.

terrestrial: Growing on the ground.

truncate: Appearing cut off at the end.

umbo: A pointed or rounded elevation a the center of a mushroom cap.

uniseriate: Arranged in a single row.

universal veil: A layer of fungal tissue that completely encloses immature stages of some mushrooms.

veil: A layer of fungal tissue that covers all or part of some immature mushrooms

ventricose: Swollen at the middle.

vermiform: Wormlike.

verrucose: Warty.

villose: Coated with long, tiny, soft hairs.

viscid: Sticky or tacky.

volva: A typically cup-like sac that remains around the base of a mushroom stalk when the universal veil ruptures.

warts: Small patches of tissue that remain on the top of a mushroom cap when the universal veil ruptures.

INDEX

INDEX